Cycles

A Journey To Purpose

A Novel By
Brett Johnson

Cycles

A Journey To Purpose

a novel by Brett Johnson

ISBN 978-0-9826962-2-4

Published by

Indaba Publishing, a division of

The Institute for Innovation, Integration & Impact, Inc.

Contact Information:
1-866-9INDABA
info@inst.net
www.inst.net

Book Cover and Graphic Design by Huey Nguyen and Connie Cheung

DEDICATION

This book is dedicated to my mom;
Margaret Kathleen Johnson,
formerly Green,
known to many just as "Ma."

Cycles

Table of Content

Cycles

CHAPTER 01

Mark Green

Mark Green edged his car into one of the empty parking spaces in front of his business. He was proud of the business he had built. When Mark started Green Cycles nine years before, he had no idea whether his products would sell. Now the revenues had grown to $75 million. He employed 225 people, and he had built camaraderie in the business, calling them "The Green Machine Team." While they had experienced some touch and go years, the company had turned the corner to profitability.

The physical plant was modern, the customer base narrow but deep, and the financial assets steadily accumulating. Green Cycles was a good corporate citizen, and had, in his mind, been forward-thinking in their treatment of staff. Living in the area loosely called Silicon Valley was fortuitous. About 50 miles south of the city of San Francisco—what locals often called "The City" but never "Frisco"—Green Cycles was on the East side of the Santa Cruz Mountains. The climate and topography made it a Mecca for cyclists who didn't mind a climb.

Mark enjoyed work, but in recent days he had sensed a cloud forming. He usually found productivity at work an antidote to introspective thinking, but more time at the business wasn't stopping the growing gray. He throttled back for a season. The business had done fine with less of his attention, and Mark figured this was a tribute to the excellent team running day-to-day operations. Having more time to himself did not make him feel any better, however. The cloud was growing, albeit ever so slowly.

A Journey to Purpose

Setting the business aside in his mind, Mark turned to his personal life. He was in his early forties, but the normal pop psychology of a "midlife crisis" didn't seem to fit. He and Teresa had been married for nearly eighteen years and had, to his way of thinking, a solid marriage. He had some regrets as a dad, but not enough "stuff" to cause the cloud. His two children, a boy and a girl, were well-adjusted, normal kids. Teresa was a great mom, and he was a predictable provider, especially given the entrepreneurial startup he had undertaken.

On his drive to work Mark's thoughts naturally turned back to his business as the probable cause. Mark was a cycling enthusiast who grew up on the Peninsula in the San Francisco Bay Area during the era when mountain biking was born. He admired pioneers like Gary Fisher, Joe Breeze and Tom Ritchey; but he found a gap in the market. His background as an engineer had proved useful when he developed designs carving out a niche for Green Cycles in the industry. He had built the first green bicycle made from 90% recycled materials. Green initially gained a following among enthusiasts in the Pacific Northwest, and that group had spawned a movement. The demand for "the green machine" took everyone by surprise.

Despite the good beginning, there were headaches in managing a growing enterprise. Mark spent less time with customers, did less cycling himself, and found himself embroiled in day-to-day management issues that were a far cry from his passion. The shine had begun to go off the bicycle. He was busy, but deep down he was not satisfied. On a flight to the Bay Area from Portland he noticed an advertisement for a business broker, and on a whim called the company. It had now been just three weeks since he met with Stephens & Sanchez in their San Jose offices. Carlos Sanchez was an affable man in his late thirties who smoothed over the rougher edges of Bill Stephens, who appeared to be the number cruncher. Mark spent the better part of a day with them working on a profile of the business. He had plenty of time to reflect on the good fortune the business had enjoyed, so when Mark signed the contract to retain Stephens & Sanchez, it was with some pause. Nonetheless, he was confident that he needed to at least explore a change, and with the stroke of a pen he quietly put the company on the market. He wasn't sure about selling, but he could easily see himself cashing in, and perhaps even doing some of the service related things he had parked while he focused on building the business.

As he pulled into the parking lot at Green Cycles his cell phone rang— it was Sanchez.

"Mark, we have a prospective buyer!"

CHAPTER

02

A Buyer Steps Forward

"Who is the buyer?" Mark asked Carlos.

Mark had a few things to learn about business acquisitions. First, the name of the potential buyer was not disclosed. The broker explained this was standard protocol at this stage of the process. He did not want to appear a novice but he switched off his car and asked Sanchez, "How do I know it is not a competitor just wanting the scoop on my business?"

"We have screened the buyers, and they have signed a confidentiality agreement. You have our assurance that they are not a competitor." Sanchez explained.

Stephens & Sanchez, especially Stephens, now that he thought about it, had forewarned Mark there would be a due diligence period, and if things checked out, he and the prospective buyer would eventually meet face to face. Sanchez assured Mark of his ongoing involvement but said Bill Stephens would be driving the more detailed look at Green Cycles.

Mark hung up and walked to his office on autopilot. He hardly noticed Tamara Wu as he passed through the reception area. The bamboo bicycle hanging on the wall behind the desk was a tribute to their proactive environmental stance. Early birds greeted him as he walked to his office; he usually stopped to chat with them, but today he was deep in thought.

Green Cycles was a family run business. In recent years Mark had instituted the disciplines of having a formal audit conducted, and he knew his financial records were in order. He did not, however, have a board of directors and relied instead on his managers and an informal team of trusted advisors outside the company...and his wife. Not wanting to upset them before he had made up his mind to change personal direction, he had begun the exploratory path of selling the company without consulting them. Now that Sanchez had called, it began to bother him that he had not included the team. He quickly had a conversation with them in his head. "But I am the majority shareholder, and my wife's family holds the rest of the shares. I am the CEO. I did start the company, and I cannot involve everyone in everything all the time. If we did that, we would never have grown to where we are now."

Mark pressed pause on the dualing thoughts as he stepped into his office. The idea of leaving made him ponder his good fortune. He liked the layout of his workspace. The floor was made of renewable wood, he had a regular desk made from rescued old growth redwood, and a tall desk made from glass, recycled of course, so he could stand and work on different projects. Years of cycling had not been kind to his lower back and he needed to change positions periodically. He had visited Blenheim Palace in the UK and been fascinated that Winston Churchill had a desk running all the way around the edge of his study. Evidently Churchill would move from project to project around the room, rather than moving the projects. He liked that idea. Green poured himself a glass of Odwalla juice, flipped open his Airbook, and began scanning his emails.

Stephens. He was going to need patience with the somewhat pedantic pencil pusher. His email header even pressed Mark's buttons. "URG-Need info soon" Mark thought to himself, "This man has the social skills of a customs officer...wait until I tell Teresa about him."

Then it hit him. "Teresa...she doesn't know a thing about this!"

A Journey to Purpose

CHAPTER

03

Teresa Green

Mark prided himself on being an enlightened husband. He thought of himself as better than average at communications, tuned in to his wife's needs. Teresa was not relegated to the menial tasks. To his way of thinking, he felt he bounced things off her pretty regularly. He was sure that if anyone asked she would say, "I am a real part of what Mark does... Sure I spend most of my time with the kids, but Green Cycles is our business." All of a sudden Mark was rationalizing to himself why he had not talked through the possible sale of their company. Teresa knew he was thinking about his options for the future. He reasoned that he did not want to bother her unnecessarily. "After all, I was just throwing a line in the water to see if there would be any nibbles. Besides, the fewer people who know about this the better. What if I changed my mind?"

Teresa sat across the table from Mark after the children headed to their rooms. Justin was planning a camping trip with some of his friends, and Kelly was doing research on the Internet for a school project. Teresa's mind was still on them when Mark began speaking. She was a little worried about the Internet, and wondered whether Kelly was too young to have unsupervised access. After Mark had been speaking for what seemed like a few minutes, Teresa tuned into the nonverbal cues and saw he was looking a little awkward. She then started to pay closer attention to the words. As she pushed the kids towards the back of her thinking , she heard words like "work...satisfaction...alternatives...different path... preliminary thinking..."

A Journey to Purpose

She had heard all of this before. Mark was, in her view, not having a full midlife crisis, but it seemed to be a mini-crisis of sorts. He had become more complex in the last year or two. He was less sure of himself; more idealistic. He was proud of his achievements, but not convinced they were important. He had even started to wonder more about spirituality, and intimated he had some desire for more meaning in life. He had not done the typical thing of buying a new sports car, but then again, he had so many new toys at work; and he was not the sports car type. "Perhaps he is having a midlife crisis after all," she thought as he continued talking. Mark had matured well. He looked different, but not worse than when they married 18 years before. He was a good man; he would get over it. He always did.

Teresa had other jobs to do and hadn't planned on chatting with Mark the whole evening so she got straight to the point. "Mark, we have been over this before. What are you really trying to say?" Mark shifted in his seat, looked out the window at nothing in particular, then looked back and locked eyes with her.

"I put the company on the market and we have a potential buyer."

A host of large, unformed thoughts lurched from side to side in Teresa's mind, all at the same time. Mark looked nervous and she wanted to comfort him, to tell him everything would be fine. "Wait a minute!" she thought to herself, "He did this to himself." She was no longer so sympathetic. She simultaneously felt relieved, thinking about the long days that extended into the evenings, six days at a time. Things had improved at Green Cycles, but Teresa wondered when a crisis might drag Mark back into workaholism. Perhaps she had nothing to fear after all. If Green Cycles was sold, Mark would not disappear into his work cave again. But what came out of her mouth was not nurturing, nor neutral commentary, nor relief.

"I can't believe you made this decision without consulting me!" she heard herself blurt out.
He looked uneasy and metered out: "It is not a decision, it's just a possibility."
"Who is the buyer?" she quizzed, her lips more tightly pursed than normal.

"I don't know yet."

"How did you find them?" she probed deeper.

"Through an advertisement on an airplane magazine."

"When did all of this happen?"

"I met with Stephens & Sanchez three weeks ago."

She stared at him in disbelief. "For three weeks you have walked around with the potential sale of the company in your mind and not said one word to me?"

"Teresa, we have talked about this."

"No we have not!" Each word came out of her mouth quite separately. "Did someone recommend them? Are they reputable? What if our competitors..."

"Teresa, for the last year I have shared that I am not convinced that everything is as it should be," he reminded her.

"Mark," Teresa said his name looking at him with focus, as if to admit that she ranted a little but that her rational self was back. "We have talked about your issues, but we have not agreed to sell the business."

Mark let her words sink in. For the first time he realized his wife thought he had "issues." Questions flashed on a screen in his head like images of cyclists speeding past a checkpoint on a road race. "What sort of issues does she think I have? How many issues? For how long have I had them? Do I have issues?" The next thing he heard himself saying was, "I am not the one with issues. I don't have issues, I have options." He knew it was a loaded statement and wished he could retract it before it was all the way out of his mouth. Teresa had the combination hurt-perplexed look on her face, making him suspect she was not perplexed at all, just hurt. She said nothing.

A Journey to Purpose

"What I mean is this: I sometimes get the feeling you resent how my career is going well and you are stuck with the children at home all day. So you don't want me to think about what could be better."

Teresa continued to look at Mark—dying to say, "That's stupid!"—but said nothing. She found it sometimes better just to nod her head, raise an eyebrow or look quizzical when Mark was in the middle of thinking aloud. So far, what he was saying did not make much sense. She was happy being a mother, she had a good circle of friends, she had wide interests, and she was as content in her marriage as most people she knew. Mark was a good provider and she lived a reasonable lifestyle. But as she looked at the man she had known for over twenty years she thought, "Mark has good business logic, but his emotional logic, if there is such a thing, is less acute." She decided now was not the time to react to his statements. Instead, she asked a question.

"Mark, why don't we set the matter of me aside for a while and get back to the sale of the business—what has happened, and what happens next?" Mark looked visibly relieved, as if he was back on safe ground. Teresa sidelined her misgivings, and let him unpack the story. After he had brought her up to speed her only comment was, "We will need to seek real wisdom on how to speak with the Green Cycles Team about this."

That night Teresa went to bed reflective, but not angry. She somehow had a sense there was more to the story than Mark was seeing right now.

CHAPTER 04

Due Diligence

"Well, do you know this Steven Suarez person?"

"Steady on, Teresa. It is Stephens & Sanchez—call them S&S if you like—and they are a professional firm."

Relieved he had dodged a bullet for breaking the "husbands check in with your wives" rule, Mark set off to work the next day with enthusiasm. "The Due Diligence process should be relatively easy" he said to himself as he made a mental checklist of things the buyer would most likely ask about. "Sales, cash, inventory, stability of the team..." He weaved easily through the imaginary due diligence traffic as he cycled to work on a new prototype bike he was road testing. The experience of the new light framed bike made of 100% recycled materials lifted his spirits. "My engineering team is doing a good job." For the first time a new thought came into his mind. "The better they do, the more money I get in my pocket when I sell the business." He began to wonder about the valuation of the company.

He stopped by the Research & Development Department when he arrived at work. A few of the engineers wanted to chat but he gave them polite, "not now", attention. Instead, he headed for the shower, got dressed and went to his office. It was time to start getting information ready for S&S; this was not something he could delegate.

A Journey to Purpose

Tamara all but followed him into the office. "Mark, you have some messages. A Mr. Stephens is coming over to see you." A few memories from his childhood seeped into his mind. Stephens was a balding chap in his mid-fifties whose brain was apparently in better shape than his body, but he had a presence about him, an air that made Mark think about his school principal. He sometimes wore an "I even know things you have not told me" expression. Mark's early morning elation about the shape of the company shifted to the pre-test jitters of his school years. He was wondering how deep Stephens would probe, and what he did not know about his own business.

Stephens walked into the office and cast a cursory glance at Mark's lair. He did not seem to be impressed. Mark offered a few explanations about renewable resources and Stephens feigned politeness while saying, "It must add a lot to your overhead." Mark started answering, but Stephens was still talking.

"I will get straight to the point. Your initial business profile is acceptable to the potential buyer. They asked to send a team to do the Due Diligence themselves, and Sanchez and I are in agreement. We feel that our running as intermediaries will only slow the process down, and may even result in them having to repeat some of our work."

Mark was still processing the statement when Stephens said, "They will be here next Monday. I suggest you get the Green Cycles employees together and tell them you are having visitors."

Stephens didn't leave much room for discussion, and Mark privately wondered whether he should call the whole thing off. Instead he found himself telling Stephens, "We will be ready."

"Good. Sanchez or I will bring them over on Monday."

"What are their names? What will they focus on?"

For the first time Stephens looked like he was not in control. "I do not know their specific approach as yet. But I believe they have done this before, and expect they have a straightforward process. You can anticipate them digging into cash flow, inventory, market share, future market size, your product development pipeline...all the normal things."

Stephens opened his briefcase, pulled out a few pieces of paper, and pushed them over to Mark. "One more thing: they want every employee to complete this document. It is called an Impact Assessment."

"What do I tell them?"

"Tell them it will only take twenty minutes to complete."

"But what do I say about why they are taking it?" Mark asked.

"Tell them it is the kind of assessment that Green Cycles should have been taking all along." Stephens was not oozing empathy.

Mark's mind shifted to some of the employees who did not know that much about the business. What would they contribute? Then there were some who were smart, but new to the company; he could probably leave them out.

"Just a reminder," Stephens said, "every employee has to complete this. It doesn't matter how long they have been here or what their grade level is. To ensure confidentiality, I have left a lock-box at reception with Tamara, and they are to put their assessments in the box. I will collect them on Friday at 3:30 p.m. and send them off to the Due Diligence team."

Mark glanced down at the assessment form in his hand. *"PURPOSE – The company's Purpose is defined. 1 to 7"* Perhaps this was not going to be as easy as he thought.

Stephens had one more thing to say before he left. "Sanchez no doubt covered this with you, but we need a Director's Minute with a sign-off from all shareholders that you are willing to be bought out, if the terms are right, of course. I have emailed you a draft resolution. You will find it in your inbox."

With that, he half-waddled, half-barreled out of the office. Mark suddenly got the feeling he was in deeper than he thought. This was more than a line in water—it was a commitment to a three week fishing expedition.

The rest of the morning was taken up with meetings with Engineering and Marketing. A luncheon appointment with a major customer who had a chain of specialty cycle stores in Oregon took him into the early afternoon. Mark got back to his office at 1:15 and found a plain white legal sized envelope on his desk. There was no address or markings.

> *Dear Mark,*
>
> *Raj and I look forward to meeting you on Monday. We will head up the Due Diligence team. We have been impressed with what we have gathered so far from your website, particularly the customer reviews. We have compiled what we call a "10-P Profile" summarizing key areas of your business. The profile is attached, and we will expand it when we speak with you. We look forward to gaining further insight from you.*
>
> *We would like to make some things clear before we begin. We are not committing to purchase Green Cycles. As independent consultants, we only recommend businesses for the buyer's portfolio where there is a strategic fit, and where the business has a solid foundation. Second, we will not just analyze the traditional things distinguishing one company from another, but we will take a well rounded look at the organization. The final thing is this: if we decide to not acquire the business, we will still leave you with recommendations for increasing the impact of your company.*
>
> *We will see you on Monday.*
>
> *Skylar*
>
> *PS: Raj is the foundations man, and I am the purpose person.*

Mark held the paper in his hand. Some aspects of the letter puzzled Mark, but it also gave him an idea.

A Journey to Purpose

CHAPTER

05

In The Light

Mark didn't want to make things seem too ominous so he called an impromptu company meeting at the end of the day. Green Cycles was proud to be a company that did its manufacturing in America. Conventional wisdom was that this would make prices higher, but with increasing gasoline prices, shipping had now become a greater part of products made overseas, and they were seeing some benefit from their "Made in the USA" strategy. The factory was a wonderful combination of lean and creative. The team took pride in their work and they were allowed to show some individualism in the way they added character to their particular sections of the operation. Mark turned a blind eye to some of the décor, which would be a nice way to describe some of the calendars, and prided himself on making all sorts of people feel part of the family. Most meetings took place standing up, and this one was no exception. Mark gathered the Green Cycles Team inside the oval of the mini cycle track employees had set up as an indoor exercise ring.

He looked out across the people with mixed emotions. Some of them had been with him since the early days of the business. He had dreaded telling them he was thinking of selling the company, but the letter from Skylar, whoever he was, had given him an idea. He addressed the team.

"We have had an excellent start at Green Cycles. We pride ourselves in a quality product and a healthy work environment. Our customers have rewarded us with steady sales growth, and we have managed to remain pioneers in a tough industry. But I believe there is more, so I have enlisted the assistance of a team that will examine facets of our business and give us suggestions for improvement. No doubt many of you have ideas for what could be done differently, and you will have the opportunity to share these. The first step the visiting consultants have requested is that each of us complete the questionnaire Tamara will hand out shortly, and return it to her by Friday lunchtime."

Mark was feeling good about his small speech; he was getting a message across.

"Sir, when will they be here?" asked Hui Han, an overly respectful Chinese gentleman.

"They will be here Monday," Mark answered graciously.

"How long will they be with us?" asked Jose.

"I estimate two to three weeks" Mark replied.

"What exactly will they look at?" This was harder to answer, but Mark remembered something about foundations.

"Think of it this way, they will start with the foundations, and work their way to the roof." He wasn't quite sure what he was saying, but it sounded plausible, and a few people nodded.

"Will there be more meetings...how will it impact our daily work...will I need to talk to them...what is their expertise...?" Mark did not know, but guessed.

"I am sure there will be more meetings...of a variety of kinds. I will let you know about this next week. Meanwhile, if you can complete these forms called..." He looked to Tamara who said, "Impact Assessments."
"...called Impact Assessments and drop them in the box near Tamara by Friday afternoon that would be great."

Someone asked, "Are they anonymous?" For a moment Mark became defensive. Was he asking whether the Due Diligence people were anonymous, or were the forms anonymous? He hardly knew the people's names, he didn't know what company they represented. Taking a form from Tamara he glanced at it and said, "No, the assessment is not anonymous; you need to put your name and some other details on the form." Tamara interrupted.

"They are not anonymous, but they are, like, confidential. The team coming in will know who you are in case you have great ideas and, like, they want to know more, but Mark and others in management will not, like, know who answered what." Mark was reminded that Tamara's biking skills were better than her spoken English, but she seemed to know more about the process than he did. Evidently Stephens had spent some time with her. Mark decided to wrap up the meeting with a bit of a pep talk.

"Green Cycles is a good little company, and over the next three weeks we will figure out what it takes to make it a great company." People smiled, but it sounded a little shallow to even him, so he tried again. "We know what we do; we have to get a grip on why we do it. We make the best green cycling machine, but what else could we do with the business? What impact could Green Cycles really be having beyond keeping customers happy? What is our purpose?"

Mark liked his own impromptu hypothetical questions, but he had to admit to himself he was not clear on the answers.

With the team briefing out of the way he thought about a second requirement: getting all shareholders to agree.

CHAPTER

06

Who Owns What?

There is no denying there was a buzz in the business for the rest of the week. While Tamara knew little more than she had already said, the locked box became a beehive, and she was the queen bee of the lobby. A steady stream of Impact Assessments slid into the box, and Tamara somehow took delight in each one. "Thank you."

Mark quickly realized he had to complete the assessment himself in order to be able to address any questions that came his way. There were 40 statements which had to be rated twice, once for actual performance and a second time for what was called "importance." Mark suspected this was a euphemism for the way things should actually be. The assessment gave Mark little insight into the potential buyer of the business; they seemed to have a penchant for alliteration and managed to force every category of the business to start with the letter P. Sanchez sent over a document titled "The 10-P Model." It explained that there were 10 spokes in every corporate wheel. Each one needed to be evaluated. Mark skimmed the document and promptly sent it on to his managers for distribution. There was some chatter about what each category might mean, but the new verbiage did not stop a steady flow of surveys into the lock box.

On Wednesday morning Mark went to the regular team meeting with the department heads and they briefly discussed the pros and cons of rationalizing their answers and submitting a view that represented the leadership as a whole. They decided this would be counter productive and that the consultants should probably get the unfiltered views of everyone. Even this discussion caused a little anxiety for Mark because he was thinking about posturing to maximize the value of the company, and his department heads were thinking about operational efficiency. There was another query that popped up at the meeting, and Kristoff Mueller, the head of engineering, was the one to raise it.

"Mark, just what did you mean when you asked, 'What is the Purpose of Green Cycles?'" Kristoff was what one would kindly label a "direct person." A German by background, he had worked in the US for almost twenty years, and he was an excellent engineer. Mark met Kristoff soon after starting Green Cycles, liked him, and invited him to join the business. A few years ago Mark formalized Kristoff's role as head of engineering. Two decades in the San Francisco Bay Area had not softened Kris' direct manner. There was a short list of things Kristoff did not like: pollution, waste, laziness, and beating around the bush. Knowing this about Kris, Mark knew this was not a time to fake an answer.

"Truthfully, Kris, I am not sure what I mean. We have started a good business around a healthy cause with a unique angle on things, but don't you ever wonder whether there is anything more?"

"Mark, the last time I checked, the purpose of a business was to make money, yah?" It was not a question. "What we do with the money once we have earned it is a separate matter." Mark could not argue; this was the prevailing view. But it did not address the growing feeling that there had to be more to life than running an efficient business, making money, and then spending the money on "quality of life."

After the meeting Mark dropped his assessment in the lock box then, all of a sudden, he thought, "Who are these people?" He bounded the stairs to his office and called S&S. An answering service picked up the line. "Stephens & Sanchez are away at a conference for the weekend and will return calls on Monday."

Teresa admired the Craftsman houses in her neighborhood as she took a power walk. She had been thinking about her role in the business. For the most part, she had been willing to let Mark do his own thing. In the beginning she dreamed with him, worked in the factory, did some bookkeeping, and handled administrative areas. But since the company had grown and become more organized she felt there was no formal role for her. Beyond that, she did not like corporate structure at the best of times, and Green Cycles was starting to look like a medium sized company with departments and rules and regulations. Mark had cashed in his retirement plan from a previous job to start the business. When they moved to new premises they needed more capital, so they took an investment from Teresa's parents in exchange for 30% ownership. Her folks had always been silent partners and had never questioned how Mark ran the company. They all assumed one day she would inherit their share, and the investment was "all in the family." But now that Mark was actively talking about selling the company Teresa wondered whether she and Mark should speak with her parents. She also began to think about what role she would play if she actually did own 30% of the company, today.

Teresa was what one might call a low-maintenance but sensitive person. She had good intuition, and most times her gut feelings turned out right. Generally an optimist, especially when it came to people, Teresa was learning to listen to her sense of when someone was not what they appeared to be. She had worried about some of the senior people Mark had hired. They were good technically, but they seemed to have a different value system. The problem was, when it came to the business, she did not really have a platform to share her perceptions. When she raised concerns with Mark, which was not that often, his logic seemed to trump her intuition. There was always a business need or a long resume or a recommendation from another colleague that outweighed her gut instincts.

Occasionally Green Cycles had let people go, which is a nice way of saying they fired them. Quite simply, the cost of having them outweighed the benefits of what they produced. That cost was rarely financial, and more often than not it was emotional; one could sometimes even say it was spiritual. It was as if some people were toxic to the soul of the corporation. It had little to do with their skills, and lots to do with their character. Green would have saved lots of money if her opinion had been sought and heeded. She wasn't sure why she was thinking about this now, but as Mark was hurriedly preparing for the session with Skylar and Raj—he still did not know even their last names, let alone their employer—she was pondering what it would look like if she did behave as an owner of the business. How would it change her relationship with Mark if she was less of a cheerleader and more of a partner?

Teresa got home, made herself a cup of tea and took it to the sunroom where she picked up a magazine and eased onto her favorite wicker chair. Enough of thinking about the business; she was going to have a sanity break before the children came home from school. An article caught her eye; it was a tragic story about a mother of three young children who lost her husband to cancer. Faced with the prospect of insufficient funds in the long term, this young mother decided to go into the family business and work her way up from the bottom.

The article jerked Teresa's thoughts back to her own situation and she found herself asking questions. "If Mark died, would I have to work?" "Would I sell the business, or would I leave it to professional managers?" "How would I run it if I had to do it my way?" "What would be the reason for keeping the company?"

She also began to wonder about who she would keep on board, who she could not work with, and how she might make decisions. Glancing back at the article lying in her lap she noticed the woman talked about praying. Teresa looked out at her garden. It was planted with low maintenance plants, mostly indigenous to California. Her thoughts went back to the business. When faced with big decisions Teresa would generally pray. Mark, in her mind, didn't seem to be one to pray too much. Not that he was against it, he just didn't see that it made too much difference in everyday life, so it was more of the right thing to do than something he felt he should genuinely do. To be fair to Mark, sometimes she got answers to prayer, and sometimes she did not…most times she did not. As far as her and Mark praying together went, this was rare, reserved only for crisis situations such as when Justin was really ill with pneumonia and they thought they might lose him.

"God, Please tell me if I am supposed to do anything about this business sale Mark is talking about..."

"Talk to your parents." The thought popped into her mind immediately. Teresa shook her head. Did someone say something to her? Was that God? It sounded just like a regular voice. She got up, took her tea cup back to the kitchen, grabbed her purse and headed off to fetch the children from school.

"Talk to my parents?" she wondered to herself.

When Teresa drove back home from school she was surprised to see her parents' old Buick in the driveway. "That is such an old person car," was her first thought. Her second thought was, "Oh, my gosh! My parents are here, at my house, just after I prayed. That is odd."

07

The Duo

Monday: Mark arrived early at work. He was not sure what to expect. Who were Raj and Skylar, how old were they, what authority did they have, were they data gatherers like Stephens, should he keep his cards close to his chest and wait for the big guys...? He was beyond his comfort zone, but thought about the potential payout, at best, or the low cost business advice, at worst. How bad could it be, anyway?

Tamara called Mark at 8:20 a.m. to say he had guests. Skylar and Raj were due at 8:30 and Mark had asked Tamara to hold them in the lobby for a few minutes. For five minutes Mark did nothing in particular, but he decided to make them wait. He scanned his emails; there was an Out-of-Office reply from S&S, so his frantic plea for more information on Friday had not been fruitful. He timed his entrance into the lobby for 8:25 a.m., him looking busy, but early, and the Due Diligence duo, as he was starting to call them in his mind, having to be on his schedule. He concluded they would be pretty impressed with Green Cycles. He sauntered into the lobby to find an Indian chap standing at the reception counter chatting with Tamara. He had interesting features, and Mark pegged Raj as being in his early thirties. He wore an expensive shirt with French cuffs and silver cuff links with geometric shaped stones that picked up the blue of his jeans, which Mark suspected were not cheap. His shoes were smart, but had the informal, non-leather bottoms. He wore a dark three-button jacket casually over the crisp shirt. Tamara seemed impressed.

Mark was still observing Raj and Tamara when he heard the click of heels and turned towards the restroom to see a blonde woman in a cream pants suit walking towards him. Why had he assumed Skylar was a man? He tried to conceal his surprise, but he suspected that she saw it anyway. Mark could not peg her age right away. He estimated she was five-six to five-eight, but it was hard to tell with the heels. She had a slightly upturned nose, was well groomed, and was, as best he could tell without staring, athletic. Her eyes were an unusual khaki color, and she had some smile lines that were emphasized by what looked like a recent day in the sun. She put out her hand first, "You must be Mark Green—good to meet you!" Mark shook her hand. She had a pretty firm handshake, so he concluded she could not be all business. Raj had swung around and stepped forward from the reception desk. "Nice lobby," he said, "and great to finally be here."

"Welcome Raj, welcome Skylar." He decided to use Raj's name first, even though she was the more senior. He felt back in charge. "Let's go to my office and chat, and then we can plan the day."

Skylar let Mark lead the way to his office so she could observe him. He paused a few times to greet colleagues, and they seemed to look him in the eye and genuinely engage with him. They walked past an open area with low cube walls, and clusters of desks denoting different parts of the administration. There were the quintessential we-are-international clocks on the wall with the different time zones. Skylar noted that instead of New York, London and Singapore, the names on Green's clocks read Katmandu, Burundi, Patagonia and Marin.

Several people passed them in the hallway. Once Mark introduced her and Raj as the "performance improvement experts" and another as the "impact enhancement consultants." "Thanks for completing the assessment," he told both of them. He was friendly, but seemed eager to get to his office. Skylar made a mental note to ask him who knew what about the acquisition.

She saw Raj was impressed with Mark's office. The first four minutes were taken up with explanations of renewable wood, recycled this and reclaimed that. The three of them pulled chairs around a small conference table in Mark's office while he talked. The glass wall afforded a view into the assembly line. While she listened to Mark regale Raj with stories, she observed the activities below, half listening, half looking. The décor in the factory seemed creative, but eclectic. Her nose for alignment told her everything was not as integrated as it should be.

Interrupting the verbal flow, Skylar reached into her bag for the Impact Assessment results while beginning to speak. "Mark, thanks for having us here. This looks like a great environment. As I mentioned in my letter, we are embarking on a process that could take two to three weeks, depending on what we find. The outcome could be any number of things. As we understand it, you have a good business, but you are not sure what you want to do with your life going forward." She deliberately looked into his eyes when she started the part about not being sure what he wanted to do with the rest of his life. It struck home.

Mark asked, "What makes the difference between a two week and three week process?"

"Actually, we could be done today. It depends on how open you are to taking a deep look at the business."

Raj chipped in, "If we do not make progress on the Impact Assessment then there may be no sense in us proceeding. But don't feel any pressure, as this is totally your business, and we are guests in your domain. We will only explore things to the extent you are willing."

Mark looked at the single chart Skylar placed between them on the table. It was a fairly typical spider diagram. He recognized the ten dimensions from the Impact Assessment form. A red line formed a fairly symmetrical shape along the outer edges of the chart. Within the red border a blue filament lateralled across the ten strands of the spider web to form a less even shape. Mark guessed the gaps between the red line and the blue line would be the starting point of the discussion.

Raj eased him into the analysis. "What do you notice about the chart, Mark?"

"The biggest gaps seem to be in Process and Planning," Mark offered. He looked more closely at the chart. "And I have to admit; I thought the People area would have scored higher."

"Process and Planning do seem to be noticeable," Skylar agreed with a smile. "This is fairly normal for a company at your stage of development."

"People seem to be proud of your products." Raj seemed to be the affirming type, and Mark was pleased he was also reading the good indicators on the diagram.

Skylar smiled at Mark as she said, "This is the summary level chart aggregating the results for your organization as a whole. As we proceed we will also share how each department sees the information. We have added analysis on how the tenure of your people affects their view on things." She paused to let the words sink in. Mark wondered how much the newer people and the old guard thought alike. "Of course we will also look at the differences between key people in the organization," Skylar added.

"But isn't this just about people's perceptions, rather than facts?" Mark asked.

"That's a good observation, Mark, and the assessment does indeed reflect perceptions. It attempts, however, to convert these perceptions to data, and as such, is a good starting point."

"Mark, allow me to mention two more things as we proceed," Skylar said.

"Go ahead."

"First, I noticed you described our process differently to the people in your organization. It will be important for us to know just what they are expecting..." She let the sentence taper off.

"To be honest, I did not know...still do not know...the name of your company. I did not know...still do not know...the likely outcome, so I told them you are business improvement consultants." Mark was trying to recall what else he said in the heat of the moment.

Raj looked at a document in his folder. "You also seemed to say something about the purpose of the company."

"How did you know that?"

"More than one person mentioned it in the 'Comments' section of the assessment, so we figured it must have been a topic of discussion."

"Which brings me to my second item," Skylar was examining the chart in front of her as if it was speaking to her. She was pointing to the gaps in process, planning and a few other areas. Mark was half listening to her and half guessing her age. He could normally tell more about a woman's age from her hands than from her face or clothing. She wore a classy looking silk-ish blouse under her jacket, and had a scarf with colors that seemed reflective of the colors in her eyes. The scarf was not an attempt to mask neck wrinkles, and had a pin of sorts with a white gold feather holding it together. He pegged her at somewhere before forty, but nowhere near twenty. Thirty-eight, he decided.

"The gaps we see are sometimes symptom, and sometimes cause."

"What does that mean?" Mark asked.

"Well, would you say that your planning is as bad as the assessment indicates?" Raj asked.

"Most of our planning is driven off customer commitments. We bring out a new model of cycles, show the prototypes to customers, they make advance commitments, and we make to order with a relatively slim overrun to accommodate direct sales." Things sounded pretty organized the way Mark explained it, and it was generally a predictable process. He went on, "The level of orders drives the purchase of raw materials, and also our manufacturing costs. So it is not that much of a mystery."

Raj and Skylar made no comment. They let Mark's explanation stand for the moment and shifted in unison to talk about people. Skylar spoke first. "Mark, you seem to have created a family-like environment at Green Cycles. Tell me about it."

"I love my job, and I want the Green Team to enjoy their work too. Of course, work is work, so not everything is fun."

"So, tell me more about the family environment," Raj said.

"It is more of a team than a family, actually. This analogy speaks well to who we are."

"How would you describe the camaraderie of the team at this point?" Skylar asked.

Mark knew they had some data he was not privy to; the question was not coming from mere curiosity. "Well, I suppose there must be a challenge or two if the scores are lower than I expected. I am surprised since we pour so much into our people."

Skylar spoke again. "Your lower scores on people may not actually have much to do with people."

Mark tried not to look too perplexed as Raj picked up the thread. "The assessment indicates people are not too sure why they are working."

Internally Mark began to bristle. He had great people, but many did not have excellent skills when he first hired them. Some of them might have struggled to get work elsewhere. There was not an abundance of good engineering and manufacturing jobs in the USA. Shouldn't they be grateful to have work? He tried not to let his irritation show. Business is business. We work to make products that people will buy so that we can make money. This provides jobs, people earn a salary, and they live life. He wondered, 'What do they mean by people not being sure why they are working?'

"What do you mean they don't know why they are working?"
he asked aloud.
Skylar smiled at him, "What is the purpose of Green Cycles, Mark?"

"Most people say that the purpose of business is to maximize shareholder value..." He was digging back into his business school reading.

"But what do you say the purpose of your business is?" she asked again.

Mark got back on the defensive. "Skylar, I am not sure what this has to do with our people," he said.

Raj stepped in: "It might not have anything to do with the lower people scores, but people want to know why they are working. Beyond that, your team as a whole needs to know why they are in business. So, what would you say is the purpose of Green Cycles?"

Mark refocused his thoughts. "The purpose of Green Cycles is to design and deliver the most environmentally advanced cycles in the world." Skylar and Raj seems impressed, so he went on. "It is about a product, and it is about the earth." His own answer sounded good to his ears, even though he had not articulated it that way before.

Skylar seemed to gather the information and store it away in a file in her mind. She looked, for just a moment, almost professorial as she folded her papers away. She paused as if she was wondering whether to share the next piece of information with Mark. She had his attention.

"Mark, we have no question this is a good company. Not every good company fits into our portfolio, however, so we need to assess whether our purposes are aligned." Mark had almost forgotten he knew nothing about who they were. "Sometimes we work with business owners who are willing to adapt their purposes to ours. Sometimes the core identity of the business simply does not fit. And a key to all this is the question of why you are in business."

Skylar adjusted the feather pin on her scarf. She did not wait for him to respond before she asked the blunt question. "Mark, why are you in business?"

Mark's mind went back to a recent conversation with Teresa. He had asked himself the same question when thinking out loud as they discussed his career. In the beginning it had been fun—a novel product, the thrill of finding customers, a tightly knit team. Now he was doing things that were less and less aligned with his passion, and the headaches of the growing company were robbing him of the joie de vivre.

A Journey to Purpose

"I used to know why I was in business..."

Raj had been quiet for a while, occasionally fiddling with his cufflinks, sometimes perusing the factory from his perch in Mark's office. Now he looked at Mark and asked, "What were the good reasons back then?"

"To grow myself as a person, to create a product I and others would enjoy..."

"That sounds good so far," Raj nodded with approval, "and...what else?"

"Well, I obviously worked to provide for my family." As Mark said this he observed the eager—perhaps even encouraging—looks on their faces, as if they were drawing him out to say more. But there wasn't much more. He liked cycling, he liked business, he liked coming up with product ideas...and he did not like bookkeeping or payroll or administration, and he was spending more and more time doing the mundane and feeling mediocre. Then a mini-panic hit him: these people weren't therapists, but business analysts. Perhaps their line of questioning was to see how focused he was on the business. He decided to go on the offensive.

"Business is all about focus," he told them. "If you take your eye off the ball, you lose focus. We deliver an innovative product to happy customers at a decent markup, and our people have a fun work environment."

"Like McDonald's." Raj said it matter-of-factly, as if there was no arguing his point.

Mark was offended at having his eco-friendly cycles compared to hamburgers.

"What do you mean, 'Like McDonald's'? They offer low cost junk food!" Raj said nothing, but instead just smiled at Mark.

Skylar leaned toward the table. "Mark, we are discussing the purpose of the business. Raj has a point. Many companies make a halfway decent product, provide employment and 'have fun' at work, whatever that means." She went on, "Are you a cyclist who is in business to support a sports passion?"

"Or perhaps," Raj appended, "it is not about the bikes, but about something else, something bigger. What if you were not making eco-bikes? Would you be doing something environmentally related?"

"The environment is a big issue to a lot of people," Mark responded, still not clear where the questions were going.

"But is it your big issue?" Skylar asked.

Mark knew it wasn't totally about the environment. There was more within him, but he was having a tough time putting it on the table. Besides, until he knew more about them he was reluctant to bare his soul. Perhaps he should speak with Teresa first.

"Mark," Raj punctured his thinking with a question. "Do you have the signed Directors Resolution stating that a majority of shareholders is willing to sell?"

"It's on its way," Mark said. He was the majority, so it would not be a problem.

"That's enough about the purpose of the business for now." Raj said. "We will dig into the Impact Assessment again later. How about taking us on a tour of the factory?"

CHAPTER 08

Two Minds

By the time Mark arrived at the house he was having second thoughts about speaking with Teresa. She had a penchant for ignoring the complexities of the business while drilling to the core of the matter. Since he didn't really know his own mind, he was reticent about opening up a tunnel that went nowhere.

"So, how did the diligence thing go?" Teresa asked while she prepared dinner.

"Fine." He decided to opt for the nonchalant male answer and let her dig if she wanted more information. He could see her debating with herself whether to press in. Instead she suggested he help Justin with his homework. Mark was relieved to have the distraction.

Over the meal Teresa said, "By the way, my dad got back to me, and he thinks you should do whatever feels right."

"And?" He could tell she was not finished.

"And mom says she thinks you are making a big mistake. So I told them to speak with you."

"So does this mean they do not agree with the sale?"

"Pretty much." Teresa didn't seem to be bothered by her answer.

Mark had thought getting an agreement from Teresa's parents would be a formality. They were not aware it was a requirement, but all of a sudden he felt a little leery about the upcoming conversation with the in-laws.

Teresa's parents were affable people. They looked like the quintessential old couple who took the happy fork in the old age road. But they did not settle on this path without give and take. Joe had worked in less-than-fulfilling jobs for most of his life. He had learned to make the most of his middle class existence by developing a knack for mixing contentment with caution.

Vera was a different kettle of fish. She was more of a risk taker when it came to finances, and was not afraid of exploring new opportunities. Vera had grown up in a well-to-do home on the East Coast. Her father had been a serial entrepreneur and she had inherited some of his instincts as she watched different businesses fail and succeed. Fortunately the wins had outstripped the losses, so Vera was not a naysayer. As a woman growing up in the 1950s she had not exercised this entrepreneurial bent in a business context. In conversations, however, her eyes sparkled more when she discussed business opportunities than recipes. Vera had supported Mark's dream when he decided to start Green Cycles. She was understanding of the long hours, and empathetic to the challenges of a start up. Mark knew her well enough to realize, now that he thought about her response, that she would not be supportive of decisions that might jeopardize the company.

It dawned on Mark he was not relishing the thought of talking things through with his in-laws. Without them he could not get the shareholder resolution signed, so he would have to bite the bullet. Since email was not an option with them, he called to set up a time to talk.

"Joe, this is Mark. How are you?"

"Mark, I'll get Vera." Mark had not even asked for her. Clearly this was going to be harder than he thought. About 20 seconds later Vera came on the line.

"Mom..." he seldom called her Mom... "I was wondering if Teresa and I could stop by for tea on the weekend..."

"Mark. Let me be straight. This is about the sale of the company, right?"

"Yes it is."

"Meet me at the factory at 9:15 on Saturday morning. If it's about the business, let's meet at the business." She left him no option.

"Nine-fifteen it is, then." He hung up.

Mark was a little irritated when Teresa came through to his study. "Have you been speaking with your mother?" he said more than asked. Teresa shrugged, not too phased by his attack, and not giving an indication of how much they had spoken.

"What did mom say?" Teresa asked.

Mark collected himself. "She wants to meet at the office on Saturday morning."

"Why the office?"

"Because it is a business meeting and she wants business to be business. I have never heard her speak with this directness before..." Mark trailed off.

Teresa was no stranger to Vera's direct insights. If she thought something was stupid, she was not one to beat about the bush. Teresa did not think Vera's objections would amount to much, but she was glad her mom was going to ask some tough questions. This was a big decision. Mark had better come up with some good answers by Saturday.

Setting the subject of Vera aside, Teresa sat down on a chair in Mark's home office and asked, "So, how was your first day with the Due Diligence team?"

"I think I handled it pretty well."

"Did they tell you the name of the buyer?"

"Not yet."

"Do you like them?"

Mark thought, "This is such a Teresa question! What does it matter if I like them?'"

"I don't know yet. The young guy, Raj, seems nice. The other one is harder to read."

"What's his name?"

"It's a she... Skylar." There was a pause when Teresa said nothing. She seemed to be watching him to see if his face revealed anything more. When she was assured it did not, she went on.

"How old?"

"Hard to say, really. I am guessing late thirties. She seems competent."

"What did they cover?" Teresa probed a little more.

"Some assessment or other, and then we did a factory tour."

"Any tough questions?"

"Nothing technical. They seem a little preoccupied with the purpose of the business...not sure why."

CHAPTER 09

An Old Model

Mark was shocked to find an old bicycle in his office when he arrived on Tuesday morning. It was dusty, the tires were cracked, and it seemed like it had been in a wreck. The frame was bent and the front and back wheel were two or three inches out of alignment. Mark's attention was fixed on the bike; a look of semi-disgust had crept onto his face as he wondered who on earth would have placed the bike in the middle of his office.

"I picked it up on the side of the road," Raj offered as he stepped forward from the side of the office. "It was probably a pretty good bike somewhere in the distant past."

Mark had not seen him standing there. "What is this relic doing in my office?" Mark asked. He was not overly amused.

"After our conversation yesterday I thought we needed a visual aid," Raj explained.

"Why not take one of our cycles?" Mark asked.

"Well, they look a little too perfect," said Raj.

Mark took another look at the old bike. He began to suspect that Raj had doctored it a little before bringing it in. The handle bars were pointing in the wrong direction. Spokes were missing. There was rust on the chain, and it looked as if someone had taken a hammer to the frame.

"What's wrong with this bicycle, Mark?" It seemed to be a rhetorical question and Mark was reluctant to give a literal answer in case he dug himself into a hole.

"Are you serious?" Mark asked. "Do you really want me to tell you?"

"What I really want to know," Raj offered, "is what makes a good bike, and what stands in the way of this old relic, as you called it, being a great bike?"

Once Mark realized there was going to be a meaningful discussion, he settled in to the conversation.

"Well, Raj, it depends on the purpose of the bike. There is no one-size-fits-all."

"Tell me about the purposes of bicycles, Mark."

"Before I tell you the purpose, let me give you a little history. Bicycles as we know them today evolved from a series of inventions by Germans, French, Scottish and American enthusiasts. The first bike had no pedals, and was known as a hobby horse, a push bike, a Dandy Horse, or a draisine. Invented by the German Baron von Drais, it was introduced to the public in 1817 in Germany and in 1818 in Paris. Sitting astride the bike one moved it along by pushing on the ground."

"So, there were no pedals?" Raj asked.

"Pedals were contributed by the French about 40 years later. They added a crank with pedals connected to an enlarged front wheel. You may be familiar with Penny Farthings."

"I have seen them making a comeback," Raj offered.

"Yes, but what you see today is a far cry from the original retronyms, as they were called. They were wood and iron constructions that were literally called 'bone shakers.' The high seat made them unstable."

Raj noticed that Mark was fairly knowledgeable about the topic, so he prodded for more information. "When did the rear wheel become a factor?"

"In 1869 a Scotsman named Thomas McCall developed the first rod-driven velocipede. Others followed, and there were also attempts to make the Penny Farthing safer."

Mark went on to explain the evolution of bicycles over time, including a discussion of specialized bikes like mountain bikes "which, most agree, begun up the road in Marin County."

"So that is why you have a clock on the wall for Marin," Raj said.

Mark nodded and went on, "You might recognize the name Dunlop."

"The tire company," Raj offered.

"That's right. Dunlop developed the first inflatable tire that made the rider's experience a lot more comfortable." Mark wrapped up the history of bikes. "In the US we view bikes as a luxury for sports or leisure. Of the billion bicycles in the world, many are the primary means of transportation, and in some cases, people depend on them for their livelihood. In Rwanda, for example, locals still make wooden bicycles for transporting products to market. So what's the purpose of a bike? It depends on how the owner uses it." Mark looked to see where Raj wanted to take the conversation.

"Mark, who is your target audience?" Raj asked.

"Our bikes are used by two groups of people: cycling enthusiasts and commuters, and in our case, both groups tend to be environmentally aware," Mark answered.

"And what is their purpose?" Raj pressed for more insight. "Why do they want your bikes?"

"I suppose they want an enjoyable life..." His voice trailed off. He didn't really know what their purpose was. He had never thought much about Green Cycles helping other people fulfill their purpose. It was enough of a stretch thinking about his own purpose.

Raj turned back to the old bicycle standing between him and Mark. "Mark, what do you think the purpose of this old bike once was?"

"This looks like an old everyday get-around-the-neighborhood bike."

"What would it take to get it back into a place where it can fulfill its purpose?"

"Scrap it and buy a new one," Mark suggested.

"No scrapping allowed: what would you have to fix, Mark? How about these buckled wheels?"

"The wheels could be straightened and the spokes tightened or replaced." Mark offered.

"And how about the seat and handle bars?" Raj asked.

"These are not your biggest problem," Mark said. "We would have to do something about the frame. It is what will keep the wheels in alignment."

"So if we fix everything else and the alignment is not addressed..."

"If you don't bring the wheels into alignment the bike will not ride well, the tires will wear, and at higher speeds the bike could be unsafe to ride."

"What about adding shocks and disc brakes to this old bike, Mark. Is that a good idea?"

"It would most likely be a waste of money. Remember the purpose, Raj. This bike is designed to get someone from A to B in a safe and steady manner. It is not a mountain bike, nor will it ever be."

"So adding bells and whistles will not make this a better bike?"

"Not really. It is what it is—a basic, everyday bike." Mark said it in a way that should have ended the conversation.

"Mark, let me tell you a bit about the framework we will be using to do the Due Diligence on Green Cycles. You will grasp it easily because it revolves around a bicycle." Raj looked at Mark to see if he was tracking.

"Go on...I am following you."

"You remember the Impact Assessment looked at 10 areas. We call these the drivers of corporate impact. They equate to the spokes on the back wheel of your bicycle."

"Purpose, people, profit and so on." Mark pulled as many areas from his memory as he could recall.

"That's right. The 10-P Model is a way to examine the spokes on the back wheel of the bike. They need to be in pretty good shape for the organization to function well. Mark, how often should one tune the spokes on a high performance bike?"

"Raj, we call it truing a wheel, not tuning. A bike gets a tune up, but wheels get trued. A good rider will notice when a wheel is out of true, or bent."

"So how do you fix it?"

"It is rare that spokes actually break. What happens is wheels get bent, and by hanging a bike on a rack, spinning the wheel and eyeballing the wheel as it rotates, you should be able to see whether it is true. A minor bend in the wheel is easy to fix."

Mark went on to explain how the spokes connected to the bent portion of the wheel could be tightened and loosened until the wheel was true. "The correct tension on the spokes can be more of an art than a science if you are doing your own repairs."

"So truing a wheel is fairly simple."

"There are exceptions. If a wheel is badly damaged then the adjustments to the spokes might cause them to protrude into the rim, in which case they could puncture the tire. So if you are making extensive tweaks to the spokes it is best to take the tire off, make sure there is no excess spoke length, and trim it off if needed."

"So fixing one thing can cause problems in other areas?" asked Raj.

"Exactly."

Raj changed his line of questioning. "Which spokes are most important?"

Mark looked a little perplexed. "Raj, it is not about the individual spokes. It is about the wheel."

"Got it."

"Mark, let me tell you a bit about the front wheel. Thus far we have done a brief assessment of the back wheel of the bicycle. You will recall the charts we showed you looked a bit like a wheel with 10 spokes. Well, there is a similar assessment we would like you and key members of your management team to complete, and it looks at the front wheel of the bicycle."

"What is the front wheel?"

"The back wheel is really about competence—how well you do the organizational things. The front wheel is about character."

"You mean ethics and things like that."
"Yes, it includes ethics, but there are 10 drivers of personal impact equally as important as the spokes in the back wheel. They go well beyond what you might think of as ethics."

"Wouldn't the back wheel be more important in the business setting?"

"I can understand your perspective, but how would you like to go back to the penny farthing? More to the point: would you compete against modern cycles with a unicycle?"

"But don't different industries need different emphases?" Mark asked. "How can you say they are both important?"

"Mark, think back to recent corporate scandals: were they back wheel problems or front wheel problems?"

"Front wheel... back wheel... maybe both."

"You are right—it is probably a mixture of both. I am sure you agree it was not just an issue of competence. Companies can be competent at bad things."

"Let's get back to the bicycle," Raj said as he placed his hands on the frame. "What do you suppose the role of the frame is?"

Mark knew that Raj was now talking about the business. "I suppose the easy answer is that it provides structure—it holds everything together."

"Pretty good, Mark. What is it that holds everything together in your business?"

Mark thought for a moment. The honest answer seemed to be the right answer.

"Me."

"You?"

"Yes, me. I am pretty much the frame that holds the different components together." Mark felt his straightforward answer was the way to go. He had founded the company. He came up with many of the initial product ideas. He had built relationships with many of the major customers. People came to him with their problems. And at the end of the day, he carried the can financially.

A Journey to Purpose

Raj looked quizzically at Mark, his head cocked to one side as if he were weighing Mark's statement. He hesitated before speaking.

"Mark, I believe you believe what you just said. That is unfortunate. I am not sure we are that interested in buying a business that is held together by one flawed human being."

Mark was not hurt by what Raj said, mostly because it did not seem as though Raj were trying to score points or win a battle. He simply looked like a man who had stumbled upon an unfortunate truth. Mark did not respond.

"Mark," Raj went on, "there has to be something bigger than the founder holding a business together if it is to create value over the long haul. I want you to think about the contribution of each of your management team and which of them you could and could not do without."

"When would you like to know by?"

"Take two or three days to think about it. I would prefer something in writing; that way you will think it through more clearly."

Mark was not an "in writing" kind of manager. He even had slogans people had bought into reflecting his aversion to long reports. "Less is more." "Less paper, more power." "I want answers not reports." But something about his answer to Raj was not acceptable, and it was clear Raj wanted a better response.

"I'll write something up," Mark offered. Then, just to test the waters he tagged on, "You are not thinking of getting rid of some of the people, are you?"
Raj just shrugged and asked, "Mark, which parts of this bike are dispensable?"

Mark immediately thought to himself, "Have you forgotten the discussion on purpose? It depends what you want to do with the bike."

A Journey to Purpose

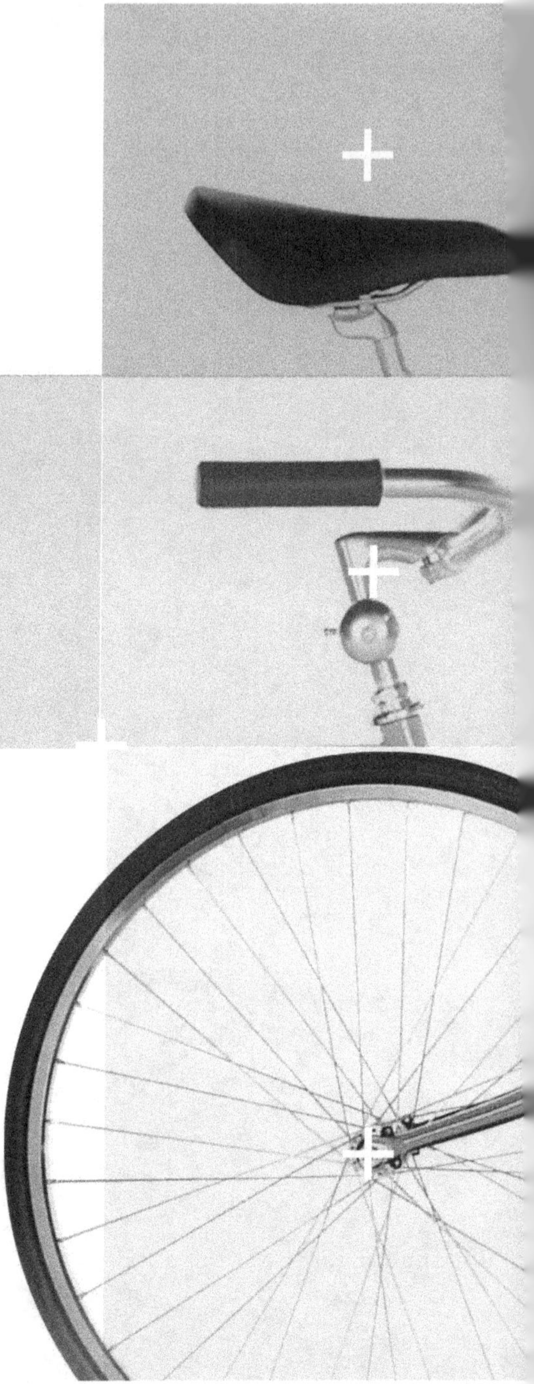

CHAPTER 10

A Matter of Alignment

Wednesday morning: Mark arrived at Green Cycles well before anyone else. He had the homework assignment from Raj, plus he had some personal reflection to do. The dead bike had now taken up residence, it seemed, and would no doubt be the focal point of many conversations. Mark was already thinking through the quick fixes that would make this relic a useful bike to someone. He thought about picking up some other damaged bikes, scavenging the parts, and quickly making it roadworthy. He contemplated whipping it down to engineering and having them do a quick fix: true the wheels, straighten the frame, add new tires, brake pads and a lick of paint... He thought about getting a handful of bikes designed to meet different needs. This would show the purpose people he knew more about purpose than they gave him credit for. Mark decided to not tell them his plan. This was going to be fun. He was going to take a pick-up, swing past Goodwill, call his buddies at a few of the old bike shops in town. Pretty soon he would be back in the driver's seat.

Tamara Wu called from the front desk at 9:55 a.m. "Bring them up to my office." Mark issued the instruction like a man with a mission.

Tamara was a little taken aback. She had worked at Green Cycles for several years and she had never heard Mark bark an order like he was commanding troops on a battle field. What was happening with him? Then it came out of her mouth.

"What's up, Mark...like, what was that?"

Mark simultaneously could not believe what he had heard, nor what he had said. "Sorry, Tamara. I was preoccupied. Would you mind walking them over to my office for me? Thanks."

Tamara's response brought Mark back to reality. Then he wondered, "Would these buyout guys see her as dispensable?" For the first time he wondered whether this process was fair to his staff.

Tamara arrived at his door fully recovered. In fact, she was sparkling a little. Clearly she had relished the opportunity to glean what information she could from Skylar and Raj and to offload pearls of wisdom. Mark made a mental note to fetch Skylar and Raj himself next time. It seems they had picked up that Green had switched casual Friday to casual Thursday to allow the Green cyclists to take an extended lunch before the roads got busy with weekend traffic. Both Skylar and Raj looked a little more relaxed, and he was touting a gym bag.

"Working out?" Mark asked as he shook his hand.

"No—I am going cycling with some of your team over lunch time. Should be fun."

A lot of thoughts went through Mark's mind. How did he know people cycled at lunch time on Thursdays? Who was he going with? Would he speak with them? What would they say to him?

"That's nice." He gave the quick polite answer, and Raj took it at face value.

"Welcome, Skylar. How are you?" He asked the question that was not a question and she did not answer, but instead go straight to the point.

"I believe you and Raj spoke about the bicycle yesterday."

"Yes, I enlightened him on the history of bicycles." Mark hoped he didn't sound too pompous.

Mark had easily understood the basic model that Skylar and Raj were using. It seemed pretty straightforward. He was beginning to feel that the devil was in the details, however, and there was a lot they had not spoken about. Skylar interrupted his thoughts.

"God is in the details." When Skylar said this Mark was shocked. Had she read his mind? Was this just a coincidence?

"That's strange," he said, "I thought the devil was in the details."

Skylar gave a professional smile, not one of the warm, from-the-heart smiles, but more the courteous smile of a doctor doing the rounds, or a pilot greeting passengers. She said, "We shall see—perhaps he is."

"What details did you have in mind?" Mark asked.

"Mark, earlier you explained the importance of alignment. Tell us about the alignment of Green Cycles. How well do you think the company is aligned?"

"I think it is pretty well aligned, actually. Raj and I talked about making sure that the front wheel—the one with all of those character things—and the back wheel are aligned. I think our people have a pretty good work-life balance."

"So you would say that they balance their work and their private side pretty well?"

"I would say so. They seem to enjoy work, and most of them have plenty of time off to do their thing outside of work."

"Balance is important on a unicycle, Mark. If people have a work unicycle and a home unicycle, balance is important. But the team that works here are two-wheel people."

"Meaning..."

Raj decided to add an angle that was a little less direct. Skylar was driving Mark into a corner and Raj was sure it was not going to be productive.

"Mark, how do you think Tamara is doing in her studies?"

Mark had to rack his brain to remember that she was studying, let alone what she was studying. He recalled that she was enrolled at a local community college as the company helped with some of her fees.

Raj continued with his line of questioning. "Do you think she is considering how to use her graphic design skills here at Green Cycles?"

"That's it!" Mark thought. "Graphic design. He knew it had something to do with tattoos."

"That's a good question, Raj. She hasn't said anything to me about it." Mark's reply did not reveal that he had no idea what happened in Tamara's life outside work.

"Mark, she has not given it any thought. When we talked on the way to your office and she shared her passion for graphics we asked her point blank, 'How do you plan to use your new qualification at Green Cycle?' and it was clear she had no intention of staying once she had her qualification."

"I did not know that."

"So how connected are the front wheel and back wheel for Tamara?" Skylar asked rhetorically. "But more important, within the back wheel for the moment, how aligned are the things Tamara does at the front desk every day behind the purpose of the company?"

They were sitting around the table in Mark's office by now and Raj leaned toward Mark as if he were going to tell him a trade secret. "Mark, I asked Tamara the purpose of Green Cycles—how can she be aligned if she does not know why you are in business?" He let the question hang in the air while Skylar reached for some papers.

"Mark," she asked pleasantly, "you alluded to the front wheel and the back wheel being in line with each other. There is an element of alignment in this, but it has more to do with integration, and we will cover that later. Right now I would like to talk about alignment as it concerns the back wheel."

"Do you mean how true the wheel is?"

"I am not sure of the correct cycling terms, so let me explain it in business terms. We discussed how each of the drivers of corporate impact is like a spoke in a wheel. They have to be in good shape, the right tension, and doing their job of keeping the wheel straight."

"True," said Mark with a smile.

"You agree?" Skylar asked.

"No, the correct word is keeping the wheel true, not straight."

"Let me shift analogies." Skylar wanted to get away from the bicycle it seemed. "You can also think of these drivers of impact as vertebrae in a spine. For the body to function well they have to be aligned. If there is poor alignment the body experiences pain, often not at the point where the misalignment is."

Raj flipped over a piece of paper and drew a quick diagram. "The head is like the purpose of the business. Each of the other P's —Product, Positioning, Presence and so on—need to be aligned behind the purpose. A lack of alignment usually leads to an underperforming company."

Skylar placed the Impact Assessment charts in front of them again and said, "Mark, since the purpose of Green Cycles is 'there but not clear'," she motioned with her fingers making imaginary quotation marks around the statement, "it is hard to assess how well the rest of the company is aligned behind the purpose."

The casual Skylar, Mark noticed, was still pretty zipped up. She wore well pressed khaki pants, a long sleeved polo neck made of light fabric, and a non-puffy vest zipped tightly over the polo. Her jewelry was not that of a person about to go cycling. The silverish feather scarf pin was gone, but there was now a small feather on the fine silver chain around her neck. She wore semi-athletic shoes that looked more suitable for mall racing than actual exercise. He suspected that she looked casual, but she was all business. She wore a touch of makeup lighting up what might otherwise be a pale complexion.

"Mark," Skylar was speaking again, "over the course of the next week we are going to examine each of the other spokes to see whether they are aligned behind the purpose."

"In cycling terms," Raj chipped in, "we are going to look at each spoke to gauge whether the tension, the length, the condition, the placement... whether all of these things keep the wheel true."

"How are you going to do this if the purpose is 'there but not clear' as you put it?" Mark asked.

"It is not uncommon for companies to have clear business goals, Mark, but an unclear purpose. This does not alarm us unduly." Skylar traced her finger over the chart in front of her as she spoke. "We suspect some of these perceived gaps result from the purpose not being clear. We have also seen the purpose does become clearer when we discuss all 10 areas, and circle back to the purpose discussion."

"What do you do if there is not alignment?" Mark asked.

"Mark, we are here to evaluate whether you are a good candidate for a take-over, albeit a friendly one. You would expect we have our own corporate assets we will bring to bear in the situation, and these include best practices and foundational principles capturing our view of business." Skylar reminded Mark why they were in the room.

"Mark," Raj looked him in the eye as he spoke, "the issue for us is not whether everything is perfectly aligned... we already know that it is not. The question is whether the areas of misalignment are align-able. Make sense?"

"How are you going to find that out?" Mark asked. He genuinely wanted to know.

"While you work on your thoughts on the contribution of each key person in management," Raj reminded him of his assignment, "we would like to have meetings with each of the key teams. Of course you are free to be in any or all of the meetings, as your schedule permits. We think they will be enlightening."

"Where do you want to start?"

"We would like to meet with Engineering and Product Design together this afternoon. I bumped into Kristoff Mueller in the lobby this morning and he is all set for 2 p.m." Skylar slipped a calendar for the next week in front of Mark and Raj where meetings with all of the departments were outlined.

"I will have Tamara get onto it," Mark offered.

"No, Mark, I would prefer it if you and I could walk around to each group, explain the purpose of the meetings, and get their agreement on the spot. We don't have time to shuffle meetings and I want to address any objections right away." What Skylar said made sense. "Why don't we do that now while Raj tightens up the Impact Assessment presentation."

Raj watched Mark and Skylar walk out of the door and said to himself, "Vintage Skylar. This will be a walk that could change Mark's life."

CHAPTER 11

Life Story

"Tell me more about the business, Mark. What parts make you most proud?"

Skylar had long learned that asking men about business is a lot more fruitful than asking them about themselves. If you were careful enough in your approach and took long enough to listen you could find the boy with a dream inside the man with a business. As they walked around the factory Mark unpacked some of the stories that went into the making of Green Cycles. He talked about the amazing ways in which they found team members, their first major contract, and the awards they won for their green machines. Skylar made small comments but mostly just to affirm Mark and grease the conversation. After the food was on the table she turned the conversation to more difficult things.

"How about the challenges?"

"There have been two major areas that have been a challenge. Finance is the first area that has caused sleepless nights. The business has been profitable but getting enough money to finance expansion without giving up control of the company has been a conundrum. Included in the issue is deciding how big is big enough."

Skylar felt that they were finally getting beyond some of the bravado of the corporate-speak that had colored earlier conversations.

"Financing is a tough issue..." she let the sentence trail so that Mark could keep speaking. "Have you ever taken on debt?"

"Not routinely. We have had extended credit from some of our suppliers, but we have avoided long term debt. The other finance-related challenge has been keeping our value proposition clear enough so we can support our higher prices and maintain margins. People will only pay so much for green."

"How well have you been able to do this?"

"It is becoming increasingly difficult despite the growing awareness of clean tech."

"What's the second challenge?"

"People. Leading people is like balancing a mobile... the kind that hangs over a baby's crib. You get everything in balance and someone changes. It's as if some people take the semblance of stability as a cue to surface their own issues."

"Have these things been draining?"

Mark thought of himself as pretty chipper. He was an "I can do it" person. He considered the challenges he had faced as part of the game, part of what comes with starting a new company. And he had enjoyed them. But he was aware of the fog forming somewhere ahead of or behind him. He was at the age when he did not know whether the best things were still ahead, or had slipped through his fingers. If it was all good perhaps he would not have decided to put Green Cycles on the market.

"I guess if there had not been some element of wear and tear then I would not be talking with you," Mark admitted. It felt good to say it. Business could be tough.

"Sometimes the highs and lows have come from the same people."

"Like Kristoff?" Skylar inquired.

Mark paused and looked at her. "He would be one of them. Has he spoken with you?"

"No, he hasn't. But I can see that the two of you are wired quite differently and I am sure that has contributed to the uphill and downhill of your relationship."

They rounded the corner where Engineering was located. Kristoff was speaking with a few young engineers. "We still on for 2 p.m., Kristoff?" Skylar called out as they walked past the group. It was more a statement than a question. She saw no need for chit-chat with Kristoff as the meeting was set.

They came to Marketing next. Skylar felt she had crossed the border from Germany to France. The orderliness of Kristoff's well-governed world had given way to an exotic colony of green explorers. Someone had created a 3-D poster of a woman on a mountain bike that protruded from the wall. Small bicycles were scattered on desks and tables. Posters of bicycle components were all over the walls. A series of sketches of the evolution of a species from ape to man hung jauntily on a wall...all of the primates were riding bikes that evolved with them. "Very clever," she thought. The second to last picture was a crisp, modern looking woman on a very current street bike. The final bike was a green machine. The bike showed the latest technology, but the rider looked more earthy, more in tune with nature than the clean cut woman that proceeded him. The message was clear. "The green machine will take you back to your roots."

Skylar paused in front of the collage. "Mark, do you remember your first bike ride?"

"I do, actually. It was a disaster."

"Tell me more."

"I was quite young, perhaps five or six, and had long envied a teenager who lived on the same block. Almost every day he flew past my house on a red drop-handle street bike that looked like the best thing I had ever seen. It had gold trim, white rubber grips on the handle bars, and had 10 gears. I was mesmerized, and I desperately wanted a bike like that. One day I was walking past his house, which was close to our home, and I spotted the bike outside his house. Before I could think I was walking up the slight incline towards his front porch..." Mark paused to demonstrate what happened next, "...and this scar on my chin is the permanent reminder of that first ride."

The story ended when Mark got to the door of an office. A shorter, solidly built young man smiled at them from behind a front door that had been propped on two trestles to make a desk. His straight black hair looked like it would take off without the restraint of hair gel. He was tanned, had slight creases around his eyes—wrinkles would be too strong a word—and flashed a white smile.

"Skylar, meet Whizz Yamamoto." Mark was relaxed, like he was introducing a friend.

Skylar was surprised. "Pleasure...not your real name, right?"

"Right. Whizz is short for Adrian Primo Yamamoto."

"And what does it mean?" Skylar asked.

"Primo means first, and Yamamoto means the bottom of the mountain. So, 'first to the bottom of the mountain... hence, 'Whizz'."

"What about Adrian?"

"I think my parents were just looking for something that sounded American and didn't get past the A's."

"So is Primo a common Japanese name?"

"No, it is Italian. Go figure."

"So you are the first Italian-Japanese from the Adriatic that got to the bottom of the hill."

"From the Adriatic?"

"Yes, that is what Adrian means... you are a serious hybrid it seems." Skylar liked Whizz. It was clear he was both the conceiver and sketcher of the collage on the wall outside. Charcoal sketches were all over his office, and a certificate in Fine Arts from the San Francisco Academy of Arts was pinned to the wall behind his desk. It read, "Adrian Yamamoto" – no mention of Primo or Whizz.

Mark stepped into the pause. "Whizz, Skylar is here to take a look at the company. You remember the Impact Assessment...she and Raj are getting to know us a little better so the results can be interpreted within a context. Why don't you tell her how you came to us—do you have a minute?" Whizz motioned to some chairs across his "desk" as he said, "Sure...take a seat. My parents are first generation Japanese-Americans who came to California in the early 1960's. They had relatives living here who had been interned during the second World War. Still, they heard there were good opportunities in the US."

"So your parents are in their sixties?" Skylar asked.

"Late sixties. I was born later in their marriage once they had settled."

"Go on."

"I developed a love for cycling early in life. We did not own a family car so my dad cycled to work. I grew up with the aim of owning a bike, not a car. My dad often reinforced the health and environmental benefits of riding a bike over driving a car."

"It sounds like he was ahead of his time." Skylar watched Whizz's face as he took in her comment. He was wistful. Clearly he had a lot of respect for his parents.

"Do you have siblings?"

"No... the Yamamoto family line rests on my shoulders."

"And how are you handling that?"

"I am thinking about it." Whizz smiled. "That's all so far."

She changed the subject, "So how did you come to Green?"

"I bumped into Mark on Mt. Tamalpais, which some say is the birthplace of mountain biking."

"It is," Mark interjected, "at least that's what we think in California."

"Anyway, Mark was riding this totally cool bike and I was riding an el-cheapo bike I had modified. So I looked at him and said, 'Race you to the bottom.' I don't know what I was thinking, but somehow on the way down I got the sense that the race was about something more. I won. I totally beat him."

Skylar looked at Mark. He was smiling. "He did. He whipped me."

"And...?"

"And so we got chatting. Mark asked what I did, and I said graphics and fine art... and bicycle modifications. So he invited me to visit, I did a few graphics projects, and here I am today."

"Whizz has exceptional talent," Mark began filling in the gaps. "He loves the environment, and he loves cycling. Just when I met him our industry was being faced with pressure from environmental groups who claimed mountain biking led to soil erosion. Green was being asked to contribute resources to the International Mountain Bicycling Association (IMBA). Whizz did start with some graphics projects, but soon became a contributor to IMBA."

"Would you mind showing me some of the projects you have done at Green?" Skylar asked.

"Not at all." Whizz reached behind him and pulled out a binder. "This is my portfolio."

Very quickly some of Skylar's intuition was being confirmed. Whizz was not a marketing professional but a highly talented, passionate person who was part-artist, part-environmentalist, part-cyclist. As she listened to him explain his portfolio she saw a series of not-so-connected campaigns that were creative, but did not add up to a marketing strategy.

"How many people are there in your department, Whizz?"

"Just three. Penny does the placement of advertisements in various trade magazines. Rafael does graphics, and I get into that sometimes too, and Tasha writes articles including customer stories, giving ammunition to the IMBA, and telling something about our new products."

"Pretty lean and mean," Skylar said, trying to offer a compliment.

"Lean and green," Whizz smiled as he corrected her.

"What's your marketing budget?"

"If Mark likes it, we spend it. If times are tough we cut back on advertising. That's pretty much it." Whizz looked to Mark as he finished his sentence.

"Advertising runs at 2% of our budget," Mark stepped in.

"Is that the fully loaded marketing cost?" Skylar asked. "Are salaries and indirect costs in that number?"

"No... that's just direct advertising."

"Okay." Skylar decided to round things off. "Whizz, it was good chatting. Now that we have met I will mull over our conversation and set up another time to chat."

"My pleasure. Nice to meet you..."

"Skylar." She helped him out as it was clear he had forgotten her name.

"And does it mean anything?" he quipped.

"We'll save that for another time." Skylar shook his hand.

"And you can tell me about the feather while you are at it," Whizz said as he motioned with his eyes the chain around her neck.

"Sure." She smiled. "Sometime."

"Just one more thing: Whizz, if you had to sketch a picture describing the purpose of Green Cycles, what would it look like?"

Whizz thought for a moment. "The picture in my mind is three men on mountain bikes at the edge of a mesa looking down at a destination at the bottom of the valley. All three men have a different road they would like to take to get there."

"And those three men are...?"

Whizz cocked his head towards Engineering to underline his thought. "Kristoff, me and Mark."

"Interesting. I look forward to exploring your picture. Perhaps you should sketch it and we can talk about it at the management meeting."

Mark and Skylar walked towards his office. "That was awkward." Mark looked like he was eager to put Whizz's comment behind him.

"How so? Why was it awkward?"

"I was pretty convinced that Whizz and I were on the same page, then he comes out with a statement like that."

"Have you ever asked him the question before?"

"No...not in that way."

"I suspect if you asked him he would have told you long ago. I don't think he is hiding anything or nurturing a difference; he just thinks he has a different view."

"How different, I wonder? That seems to be the question."

"We shall find out soon enough." Skylar was beginning to form a viewpoint but needed to speak with Kristoff before she could outline it to Mark.

As they walked away from Marketing, Skylar turned casually to Mark and said, "Now tell me about your team, Mark. How many did you come across in a serendipitous way?"

"Well, you already know about Kristoff and Whizz. I met Cindi in HR at church on Easter. Teresa knew her. She is a single mom and needed to get back into the market after her divorce. Nice gal. She has been with us for four years. I used to do all that stuff."

"How about Finance?"

"Well, we don't really have a VP of Finance or Finance Director per se. Teresa's mom used to help me out in the early days, but now we have a fulltime bookkeeper cum Controller, Jim van Doorn. He has an interesting story."

"How did you find him?"

"I was invited by a friend to attend a business luncheon. I thought it would be a good networking opportunity, and I rarely go to these things, but this time I went. I forget who the speaker was, but Jim was there telling his story. He had just got out of jail."

Mark looked at Skylar. He wondered if she was thinking what others often asked, "And you hired some guy fresh out of jail to manage your money?"

If Skylar was alarmed it did not show. "And why was he in jail?" she asked.

"Embezzlement." Mark let it sink in. "He stole money from a company, but evidently had some form of a religious experience, and so confessed his crime. As a "thank you", they filed charges and he ended up in prison."

"So you hired him. Did you feel sorry for him?"

"Not really. I just figured anyone who has been honest enough to confess a crime and spent time in jail for it is someone who could be trusted with my money. So I offered him a job."

"So you are a pretty trusting guy."

Mark never thought of himself as overly trusting, just logical.

"Not really. It just seemed right."

"Good thinking. I look forward to meeting him."

Mark was surprised at the affirmation.

"How about fulfillment, logistics, supply chain? Who do you have there?"

"You mean the warehouse and stocks and shipping?"

"Yes." Skylar made a mental note to go back to the Impact Assessment and look at the Process P. Some of Green's areas seemed pretty current, but there were other areas where Mark's terminology was dated.

"Jake's a great guy. I met him at Home Depot when I was buying supplies for a project at home. We got chatting, he said he was a cyclist... he's one of the most organized guys I know."

"What was he doing at Home Depot?"

"He was running a section of the warehouse. Nice guy."

"Any other key hires?"

"Sometimes we advertise for people, sometimes they come to us via referrals. Staff get a bonus if they bring someone in to fill a need and we don't have to use a recruiter."

"So lots of people know people."

"As I indicated before, I think of us as the Green community."

"So it is a family business, then?"

"Not in the klugey, sloppy sense. But relationally, it is true."

"So you are a family man."

"Is that a statement or a question?"

"It's a statement. You have a good relationship with your wife and kids. You have hired some key people based on relationships, and you treat your employees as family. That's not a bad thing, Mark. Work and family can function under the broad umbrella of what we would call 'household'."

She let it sink in, then asked, "Did you think you would go from crashing a stolen bicycle to all of this?"

"I borrowed it temporarily," Mark corrected.

"You stole it and crashed it." Skylar teased him. "And now you have made it into a good story. That works for me!"

Skylar and Raj met to compare notes on their various meetings. They were following a deliberate set of discussions to gauge the veracity of what they had observed from the initial gap analysis revealed by the Impact Assessment. On the surface the three key players seemed to be Kristoff, Whizz and Mark. The rest were important but did not influence the business as much. The exact relationship of Teresa and her parents to the future of the business still had to be explored.

"How was the discussion with Mark about the shape of the bicycle?" Skylar asked Raj.

"I think he got it. But he was a little defensive when he thought I might be suggesting that Green Machines was a little rusty or out of alignment."

"Does he grasp the concept of alignment?"

"I think he gets it theoretically, but I don't think he has translated this into practical action yet. He could do it, though."

"Well, we will have time to inspect each spoke in the wheel..."

"How about you; what did you find?" Raj asked.

"I learned something about Mark. He has a good heart, and he hires by instinct."

"And...?"

"And I had a fascinating meeting with Whizz Yamamoto in Marketing."

"How is he doing with Marketing?"

"Well, he is actually an artistic environmentalist who has linked his various passions together. He is not really a professional marketer."

"Anything else?"

"I asked Whizz to paint a picture of where he saw the company. Fascinating."

"And are you going to share it with me?" Raj asked.

"After my meeting with Kristoff," she began gathering her things to leave. "I have a hunch he will shed more light."

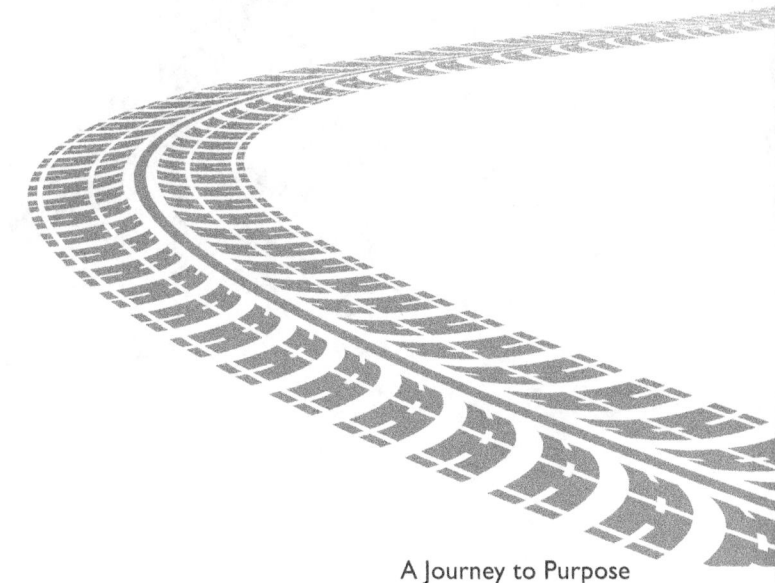

A Journey to Purpose

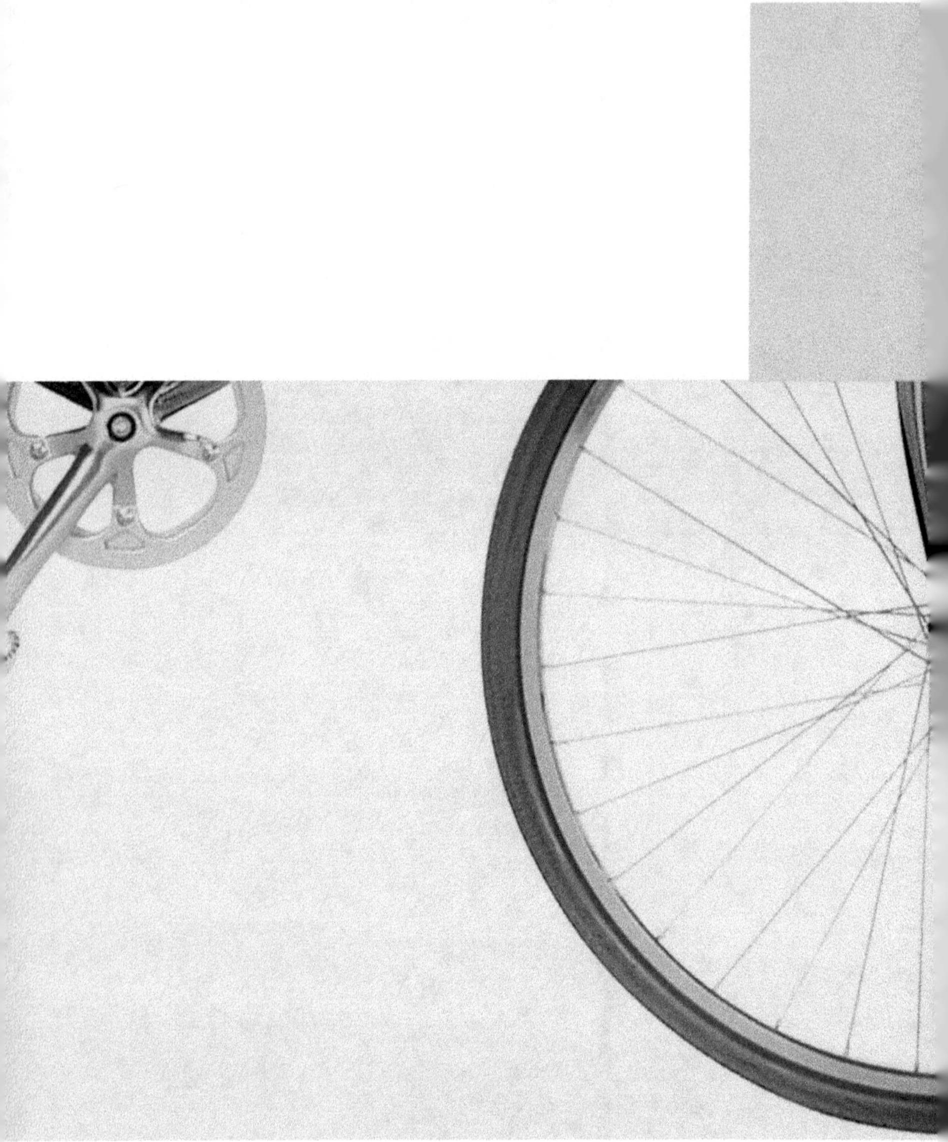

CHAPTER 12

Weed Killer

Skylar arrived a few minutes early for the meeting with Kristoff. He was in his office but looked busy. She chatted with Judi Sanders who introduced herself as Kristoff's soigneur, his cycling support person.

"How long have you supported him?" Skylar asked.

"At work, just over a year. On the road, for about three years. We know each other outside the work context."

Skylar could tell there was a level of familiarity, of knowing someone. She decided to offer the "no comment" phrase that seemed to work in these situations.

"That's nice."

She had one eye on Judi and another on Kristoff to see whether he was stalling in order to make her wait for exactly 2 p.m. Or would his curiosity about her informal dialogue with Judi draw him out of his office early? At 1:55 curiosity beat the chronometer and Kristoff marched out of his office.

"I see you have had a chance to get to know each other..."

"A little. Judi tells me you know each other quite well."

Kristoff shifted his weight around on his feet, and Skylar thought she saw his blonde goatee become more contrasted with his skin. "He is blushing," she thought to herself.

"Ja, ja. One could say that. Anyway, let's go to my office and begin, shall we?" He sounded a little more German than usual, and it seemed like he was using the heavier accent to create an unseen barrier, letting Skylar know that despite what she had learned from Judi, she was going to have to work to learn more from him.

As Skylar looked around his office she could not help but feel the stark contrast between Kristoff's icebox-type office and Mark and Whizz's relatively organic habitat. Mark's was constructed to be a springboard from which the "green machine" story could be told, and Whizz conveyed unspoken beliefs about nature and man's relationship to it through his office. As Skylar took a seat across from Kristoff at this desk it brought back memories. She felt like she had been here before. She scanned for more clues and, sure enough, there it was, a neat glass plaque with the following inscription: "Kristoff Mueller - Service Manager of the Year, Mercedes Benz 1999."

"So you used to work at Mercedes Benz?"

"Yes, well...I was trained in the Mercedes Benz way."

"And how would you describe that?" Skylar really wanted to know.

"My interpretation is if something is worth doing, do it well the first time, and if something looks like it might break, fix it before it does."

"And how has it been implementing that philosophy here?" she asked.

"Not so easy."

"Tell me more..." Skylar decided to flow with the conversation.

"In my background I am used to doing things efficiently. I don't mind the creativity at Green Cycles; anyone can see that it has been good for the company. But I like to have a plan."

"And there is no plan at Green Cycles?"

"There is somewhat of a plan, but it is only kind of a plan." Kristoff was being honest. This was the way he saw things. "Even the best creative minds at Mercedes Benz worked to a design which in turn submitted to a plan."

"Fill me in about the planning process."

"We are not short of product ideas. They seem to spring up like weeds. I then have to sift through them to figure out whether they fit."

"So you spend a lot of time saying 'no' to people. Who do you most often say 'no' to?"

"Mark." Kristoff answered without hesitation.

"Why Mark?" Skylar encouraged him to continue.

"Well, actually. Whizz has lots of the ideas, but he goes straight to Mark who then comes to sell them to me. Mark also has 'technical' or product ideas."

"And are they good ideas?" Skylar asked.

Kristoff grew irritated, as if she didn't understand. "That's not the point!" he exclaimed emphatically.

"The point is..."

"Unless there is a clear plan it doesn't matter how good the ideas are. I cannot build long term success off random brilliant ideas."

"But haven't you been successful so far using the 'random inspired ideas' approach?"

"Skylar," Kristoff began speaking more slowly, "I am talking about 'sustained success.' Anyone can be lucky when they are a small company, but you cannot grow big off small behaviors and good luck." She decided to not argue the merits of his point but to instead dig deeper into his ideal world.

"Kristoff, if planning was done your way ..."

"We are not talking about my way, but the common sense, logical way. It is the way mature businesses operate." Skylar did not mind the lecture because she was learning about his view of business.

"So if you were king for a day, what would you do?" Skylar asked the question for two reasons: she wanted to understand his thinking, but she also wanted to see whether he relished the thought of being king. His body language seemed to indicate he did, and a small orange light went off in her mind.

CHAPTER

13.1

A Common View From The Cliff

Teresa was intrigued to get an email from Skylar. This was her first contact with the Due Diligence team and she was curious.

> Dear Teresa,
> Mark has passed on your email address and I would like to give you some background on the attached email and explain why I would like you to be at a special meeting with key managers. Green Cycles, as you would have gathered, is at a crossroads. The junction looks different to the various players involved. I would like to unpack this at a meeting with Mark, Whizz and Kristoff. You need only observe, and afterwards I would like to debrief with you. No preparation is needed for the meeting and you are free to participate, but afterwards I would like to meet with you to get your take on things once the meeting is over. I think you will shed special light on the road we are travelling, and where it should be leading. The attached meeting announcement memo gives the formal background to the meeting.
>
> Regards,
> Skylar.
>
> PS: Please bear in mind that the details of the Due Diligence process are known only to you and Mark.

A Journey to Purpose

+ + + + + + +++ + +

> From: Skylar
> To: Mark, Kristoff and Whizz
>
> Raj and I have enjoyed speaking with you these last few days.
> What is still not clear to us is the real purpose of Green Cycles. We
> have scheduled a two hour workshop to unpack your purpose. No
> special preparation is needed. We will meet tomorrow at 9:30 a.m.
> in Mark's office.
>
> Skylar.

Skylar had given Mark the rationale for the workshop but had avoided his questions that would have preempted the meeting. All she had said was there were differing views of the future, and they needed to be explored. She had also insisted that Teresa be there. She represented a major shareholder block, would have a unique perspective, and was the only person, other than Mark, who knew he was contemplating selling.

"Mark, I need help getting the kids to school if I am going to make it on time for that meeting."

"Sure. I will take them."

"What am I supposed to wear?" Mark knew that his answer would make no difference to what she decided, but he had to give an answer nonetheless.

"I would wear smart casual."

"Smart casual is what guys wear. Should I wear a skirt or slacks?"

"Definitely slacks."

Teresa arrived at the meeting in a bold colored sun dress. The heels on her strappy sandals were high enough to give a sense of sophistication and accentuate her calves, but not so high as to make her appear all style and no substance. Her purse was on the large-and-functional side, but it was still fashionable. She did not look like a woman who had been temporarily dragged away from watching kids. Whizz was already in the room when Teresa arrived and he was clearly surprised to see her, but gave her a warm welcome. Kristoff arrived a minute later.

"Oh. Hello Teresa." He was less than thrilled to see her. "You are attending the meeting then?" Skylar stepped into the conversation.

"Since we are all here, let me set the context for the meeting. As you well know Raj and I have been examining Green Cycles from various vantage points this last week. Based on our meetings with you we are clear on two things: you do not have a common view on where the business should go, and second, just how the company should operate while it is still evolving. We are going to do some exercises in this workshop to try to arrive at a better understanding of your purpose. Any questions?"

No one asked a question, so Skylar proceeded.

"I have asked Teresa to join us today for several reasons. I would imagine no one knows Mark better than she does, and she can help unpack his views on things. I also expect she has lived through many of the ups and downs at Green Cycles, so she will most likely bring a long term view to things. Finally, she represents a major shareholder in the business and, as a key stakeholder, her perspective is essential. Welcome, Teresa."

Teresa had been curious to meet Skylar. It was hard to judge her age but she seemed younger than herself—probably the benefits of not having carried two kids. On the other hand, she seemed poised and mature. Teresa concluded Skylar had a timeless quality to her. Raj's white linen shirt looked good against his dark skin. Teresa put him at 33 or 34. He seemed outgoing, smart and savvy enough to smooth over the relational cracks that might come from Skylar's directness. Teresa brought her thoughts back to the meeting as Skylar spoke again.

"I had a great chat with Whizz a few days ago. I asked him to give me a word picture of how he saw the business. Whizz, why don't you share that with us?"

To her surprise, Whizz walked up to the whiteboard and began to sketch. "When Skylar asked me to think of a picture describing Green Cycles this scene immediately came to mind. The three of us guys were at the top of a summit looking down at a common destination below. It seemed clear to me each of us had a very different idea of how to get from where we were to where we want to be." Raj and Skylar were observing Mark and Kristoff to see how they tracked with Whizz. "The sense I have is we have been on the same path, for the most part, but that our views of how to take the business forward are possibly diverging."

"Whizz, I was not there, so help me understand," Raj said, "Can you expand that a bit for us: is it the speed, the route, or the approach the three of you have?"

"I don't think it's the destination, and I don't think it is the speed. Kris is pretty good at applying the brakes when needed, but he likes an adventure too. I think it is the method—how we get there."

"A business has to have an efficient, workable operating model, Whizz." Kris explained. "I sometimes think you have this 'if we build it, they will come' mindset. But if we build it, they may not buy it, and we will have over capacity."

Raj looked to Mark and asked, "Is this the picture you see? Or do you see a different picture?"

Mark looked contemplative. "I think we are pretty much together in this..."

Kristoff jumped back into the conversation. "Personally, I think we started going onto different trails some time ago. I don't see us as being together at the top of a hill. I think we are at the bottom of a long, steep climb and we don't agree on how to tackle the mountain."

Whizz took it lightly. "That's because I am an optimist and you are a pessimist."

"No, I am a realist," Kristoff corrected.

"So, I am an optimist and you are a realist?" Whizz asked.

"No," it seemed Kristoff's accent was getting thicker, "you are an idealist."

"And what am I idealistic about?"

"You are idealistic about the environment, and about the extent of the impact we can have on it."

"Okay...I'm cool with that."

The interchange between them was good natured so Skylar decided to keep it flowing and asked Kristoff, "How would you describe Mark, then?"

"Mark is a little harder to put in a box. He is part optimist, but opportunist, and part futurist. He buys into Whizz's dreams, and he sees gaps in the market that he thinks we can address, and he sometimes sees where the future will be before it happens."

"But you wouldn't put him in the realist camp, or would you?" Raj asked.

"Not even close," Kristoff said bluntly.

Mark finally entered the conversation with a question for Kristoff. "Kris, wouldn't you say that I am pretty realistic about our finances? I can tell you our sales, our margins and our cash flow pretty accurately. I can tell you our headcount and what our projections are for the next quarter, and which customers are more profitable than others."

"Let me rephrase it," Kristoff went on, "you are a realist when it comes to what has already happened with the finances, but you are a dreamer when it comes to what could happen on the product side of the business. You constantly think of this change or that addition or the next design. And I am the one that has to take those dreams and make them real."

"So my dreams become your workload."

"That's true for the products we decide to take forward. My real work, however, is sifting through the avalanche of new things to figure out what is essential, and what is a distraction. And if we are going to progress well, we have to find a way to segment the avalanche."

Mark nodded his head to acknowledge Kristoff's comment.

"Thanks, Whizz. That prompted a useful discussion. Let's change gears." Skylar reached for a small stack of cards in front of her and began handing them around. "I want each of you to take a card and reflect back on your first week at Green Cycles. Can you remember your first days here? Write down on the card what excited you about Green Cycles back then. What grabbed you?"

"Do you want me to do this too?" Teresa asked. She had been quiet until now. "I am not sure I can remember."

"It would be great for you to give it a bash," Raj encouraged. "I am sure some of the dreams you and Mark had for the company can be dredged from your memory."

"Oh, I can remember some of those," Teresa offered, "but I am not sure they bear any resemblance to today."

"That's fine," Raj replied, "that's just what we want to hear."

The management team spent some time writing on their cards. Kristoff was finished first and went to get some water. "Can I get anything for anyone?" he asked as he left the room.

Whizz's card was back next. It was illustrated. Raj looked across at Teresa and she was writing frenetically, and pretty soon asked for a second card. Mark looked like he had executive brain freeze... as if he was trying to recall the right thing to say rather than write what he really felt. Raj mused that Mark was probably experiencing the rather common founder's dilemma: how do I acknowledge that the world has changed without sacrificing my initial vision?

Raj took the cards and stuck them to a large, frosted glass wall that acted as a white board. He organized them by theme.

When Kristoff came back into the room Skylar gave the next set of instructions. "You may have guessed your next assignment is to take three cards and on each card write one word that describes how you feel about Green Cycles today."

As people worked Skylar and Raj collected the cards and began to group them in categories. Once everyone was done Raj said, "Let's take a look here... we have a bunch of cards dealing with growth, some with family, a group dealing with efficiency or control, and some dealing with uncertainty regarding the future. Excellent."

Looking at his watch, Raj signaled the end of that exercise and said, "Let's key off this last group of cards dealing with the future. Your final exercise of the day is to jot down three bullet points that should be included in the future purpose of Green Cycles. I don't need long sentences, just some key words. What would you see as 'must haves' in the future of the company? I will give you seven minutes for this, but let me know when you are done."

The team filled out cards and Skylar collected three from each person. "We are going to break these into three different groupings. First there are the personal items, what you see for yourself or for others in the company. The second group is for the business or even the industry, and the final group is for the community, or the world—outside stakeholders. So, the first one says "Family"—where does that go?"

The group began to sift through the cards, placing them in columns. Most of Kris' cards where in the business column, and Whizz's were in the last column. Mark's were spread evenly. Teresa had two in each column.

Below the surface Mark was beginning to feel uncomfortable, so he was glad the meeting was over. He was particularly relieved the discussion had not delved too deeply into the purpose of the business because he was sensing he and Whizz and Kristoff were not on the same page. He was also pleased he had not been asked to share his picture of the business because the only thing that came to mind was that of a canoe heading towards rapids with five people paddling in different directions: Whizz was at the bow, having a great time, he was at the back feigning giving direction, Kristoff was in the middle trying to keep things stable, and Teresa was kneeling on the hull trying to bail water because somewhere there was a leak. The final person was Vera, his mother in law. She had a large paddle and was paddling backwards. He was dreading his meeting with her the next morning.

CHAPTER 14

Sweet Ultimatum

Mark had not worried about a meeting with Teresa's parents for a long time. Today, however, he was concerned. Vera had become all business— no nonsense in his last few interactions with her. In one way it was fun to see the little old lady have some fire in her belly, but the disconcerting part was he was not quite sure why she had a bee in her bonnet. He was about to find out.

Mark decided to drive to the office to meet Vera. He arrived at 9:15, giving himself time to make her a cup of herbal tea and gather his thoughts. He decided the best approach was to let her talk, and he would just listen. He was sure that once she had her say she would see things his way.

Vera pulled up to Green Cycles in the Buick. The car made her look older than she felt, but it was paid for and she was not going to get some new fangled vehicle with a screen called Tomtom, or whatever it was, that told her where to go. She had taken enough direction in her life and wished she had followed her own nose more often. Pretty convinced that Mark was not seeing the full picture in this sudden move to sell the company, she intended to find out what was driving him.

Mark came to the reception area to let her in as most of the staff were off on Saturdays.

"Morning, Vera." He decided to skip the "mom" routine as she might see it as patronizing.

"Hello Mark. How are you today?"

"Great! Everything's fine."

Vera did not answer but gave him the "if everything is fine why are you thinking about selling the company" look. Still, she was courteous.

When they arrived at his office Mark said, "I made you some herbal tea. There is honey, should you want it."

"Trying to sweeten me up, Mark?"

"Actually, I am here to listen and to hear your perspectives. I know you have good business savvy."

Vera looked at him and cocked her head to one side to appear non-threatening. "Mark, I am not here to give you a lecture. I am here to help you explore all the facets of this situation. Now, you know me. I will offer some motherly advice from time to time. Since I own 30% of the company you will have to politely take it into account. I will not stop you from doing what you want to do. But I do want to make sure, Mark, that you consider all angles."

Mark seemed to relax once Vera said she would not block the sale, so she went on. "Mark, tell me how this came about." She settled back in her chair as if she was expecting a long answer. She seemed to be in no rush.

"Teresa and I have been talking on and off for a few years about our future," Mark began. "The business is going well, on the surface, but I am spending less and less time doing the things I am passionate about. As the company grows I release more of its operations to others, and instead of feeling lean and green, it feels pedestrian and gray."

"Have the sales dropped?" Vera asked.

"No, this is not really about the financial performance, but whether it is what I want to be doing for the rest of my life."

"And this isn't just the normal midlife..." she didn't want to call it a crisis, so Vera let the sentence tail off. "Teresa tells me the two of you have ruled that out."

"Vera, we spoke about that some time ago. From what I gather, midlife crises are really about identity and loss of youth. I feel great. But I do think about purpose more than I used to."

"Personally, you mean?"

"Yes, personally. The nice thing about a business is the purpose is clear: make money and build wealth by selling a product or service that meets a genuine need. It seems to have neater boundaries around it."

"Mark, did you really start Green Cycles just to make money?" Vera had a quizzical look, as if she knew this was not the case. She went on. "Think back. Were you simply trying to build a better widget and do it more efficiently than someone else so you could feed your family? That's not what I remember."

Mark had to think for a moment. Vera was right. He had not started out just trying to run a well-oiled business that generated cash. Many years ago he had harbored dreams about changing the way people thought about reusable materials, waste and the environment. Not just him, but Teresa too. Before they had kids she was in it with him.

Vera interrupted his thoughts. "Mark, here's my next question: have your passions changed since you started the company?"

"If I am honest, I think they have waned. They don't drive me as much as they used to."

"Why not?"

"Why not?" Mark was wondering whether Vera knew what his everyday life looked like. He wanted to take her to his calendar and show her how full it was. He wanted to say, "I get about 100 emails a day, and every time we hire someone the number of emails goes up, not down. I get Facebook messages from cyclists, requests for information from user groups..." He stopped himself as he thought: "She doesn't even have email!"

"Vera, I guess my passion has been buried by adminstrivia...hundreds of little administrative things. None of them on their own is a passion sapper, but taken together they make work less fun."

"Is work supposed to be fun, Mark?" She raised her eyebrows as she asked the question.

"Nowadays, Vera, people expect work to be fun. We are, after all, somewhat in the leisure or sporting industry. So people expect a measure of fun."

"So are you saying that a decrease in fun has led to a decrease in passion?"

"I guess you could say that."

"Well, if your passion is only fueled by fun it is bound to decrease sooner or later." Vera paused to rearrange her thinking and let her point sink in. Then she came at things from a different angle. "As an investor in Green Cycles, I tend to think that my return on investment will be determined more by what you are committed to than by what you are enjoying. What is the company committed to?"

Mark took a breath, tried not be defensive, and thought about the previous day's meeting. "Well, I am committed to pushing the edge on clean tech, Kris is committed to stability and efficiency, and Whizz is committed to preserving an enjoyable environment." He decided to omit "and we all want to have a fun place to work" because he knew Vera was not going to buy it. Besides, recently Kris had not been too much fun.

Vera thought Mark's answer sounded like three different things, but she decided to let him off the hook and move on to another topic. "Mark, correct me if am wrong, but I seem to remember you speaking of building a business that would be a support to you and Teresa for many years to come. You may even have talked about my grandchildren working with you one day. When did that change?"

"Vera, everyone in Silicon Valley knows good businesses have an exit strategy."

"What's an exit strategy?" Her nonplussed stare told him she did not really put much weight on what everyone in Silicon Valley embraced.

"You know, there has to be a good way to get out of the company otherwise you can't cash in and move on." The second Mark said this he realized that in Vera's world this was not the way things work.

"How do they 'exit'?"

"Companies either IPO... they go public, or they sell. In our case, I don't think it is feasible to go public..."

"To what? Move on to what?"

"To the next opportunity. Or to another investment."

"So you start something, you sell it, and you start again."

"That's one way to do it. Or you sell, and invest in someone else who will start a business."

"Mark, I think you are too young to retire."

"I am not talking about retiring."

"Sounds to me like you are. You see, we retired and put our money into you so you could have good work. Now you want to stop work and put your money into someone else."

"I would be shifting to become less of a do-er and more of an investor, which is also work."

"And would the business you in invest in keep 'pushing the edge on clean tech', as you said?"

"Not necessarily."

"So let me get this straight. You said your purpose was in clean tech, but you are willing to sell the company that enables you to fulfill that purpose and invest in another one that doesn't?"

Mark said nothing. Vera looked at the table in front of her; she seemed to have an imaginary notepad with a long list of questions. Or perhaps she was like a deposing lawyer making up questions based on prior responses.

"Mark, you know Joe and I think the world of you, but we planned to leave our share of the company to Teresa one day. You think I come from a different era, and you are right. I have to say, truth be told, if I were part of this younger generation I would not be a passive member of the team. Back in the day I would have jumped into business if there was more space for women."

"Are you saying I should be making more space for Teresa?" Mark asked.

"Not really. I think you are a good team and she has her hands full with the home. What I am saying is this is a big decision and it needs to be one you make jointly. Unless she can look me in the eye and tell me that she is 100% with you on whatever you decide, you will not get my signoff." Vera looked firm on the matter.

"Tell me more about your reasoning." Mark prodded for more insight.

"There are two types of couples, Mark. Those who watch their spouse make decisions, offer input here and there, and hope their husband, for the most part chooses well. Then there are more rare combinations who agree to not move forward on major items unless they are fully in sync. Which do you think you are?"

"From my perspective, we are in sync. We are generally together on things."

"Do you think you and Teresa are making business decisions together more or less than in the past?"

"It is different now. I agree she makes the decisions about the kids, schooling and the home, and she leaves the work decisions to me. So we have a delegation of duties, a separation of powers." Mark thought he had a good way out.

"An agreement to make separate decisions is not what I am talking about." Vera seemed hardly impressed by his response. "Mark, there comes a season when husbands and wives have to figure out how to do the big things in life together, not as adjuncts to each other. It's that, or face the possibility of drifting apart. For you and Teresa—and you know I am a non-interferer—I think you are at that fork in the road. Now I know you and she think you are in no danger of relational drift, but the way you are going about this business sale tells me otherwise."

Vera and Mark let the weighty comment with all of its potential to wreak havoc lie on the table between them. If he objected, she proved her point. If he dismissed her, the sale would be in jeopardy.

Vera reached down to pick up her purse, then leaned forward towards Mark. "One more thing. I am interested in your purpose, but I am more interested in your purpose as a couple, and how it relates to the company. Make sure you give it better thought." With that she was up and on her way to the door somewhat ignoring Mark as he said, "Good, good...I will do that."

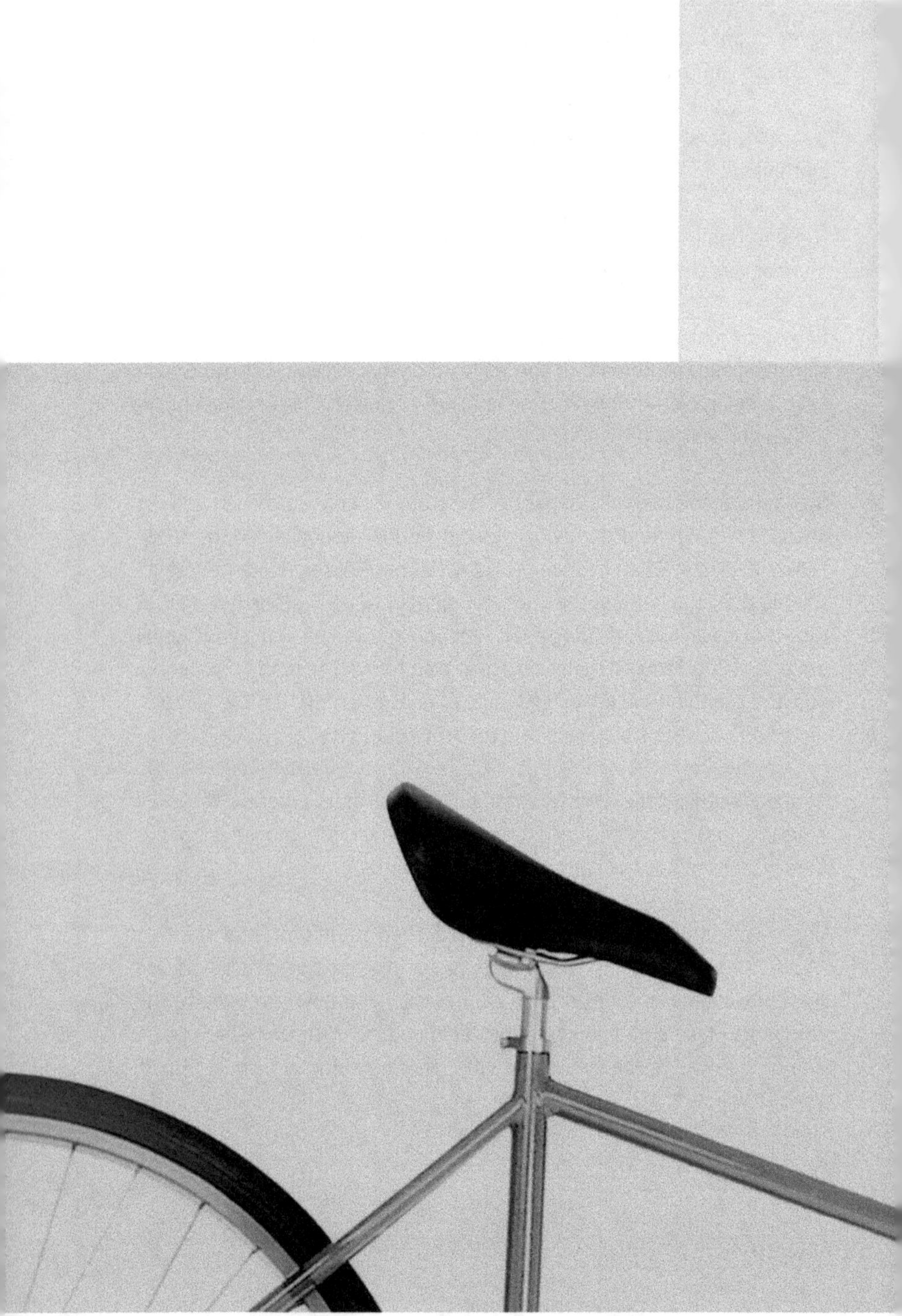

15,

Donkey and Bicycles

Sunday mornings were good times to catch up. When the kids were young Teresa had often taken them to Sunday School, but the weather in California, sporting events and the general need to have some down time had all contributed to Mark being less than excited about attending church. When Teresa raised the prospect of them going to a Sunday morning service to "get guidance" Mark felt two emotions: first, he felt it was a little shallow to just show up and ask "The Big Guy," as he sometimes called God, for help when in a pinch. Second, he could not recall ever hearing a sermon on business valuations, market penetration or cash flow management. He didn't particularly think God was into business. The problem for Mark, however, was he still had the conversation with Vera fresh in his mind, and if Vera got wind that he had turned down Teresa's attempts to work with him on the business decision, the whole process could be in jeopardy.

"Yes, dear!"

Mark felt a bit awkward; the people around him were getting more out of the preliminaries, as he called them, than he was. Singing, reading, announcements... he usually tuned out until the talk from the speaker. Even then, the topics did more to make him feel inadequate than empowered.

The front voice droned: "Today our guest speaker is going to talk about business. What is the connection between God and business? Here to speak to us today is a businessman who is also a quote-unquote 'marketplace minister.'" Front man wiggled his fingers. "To expound on what this is all about, let's welcome Ken Jameson."

The man who stepped up to the lectern looked like a regular guy in his late forties. There was nothing unusual about him, meaning, he did not look to Mark like the overly religious type. He wore khaki pants and a blue buttoned down shirt. He did carry a Bible and Mark wondered how he was going to connect the Bible and business.

"Hi, my name, again, is Ken. Usually I spend my time speaking with businesspeople in their regular place of work, but since I am in a church today I am going to read a Bible passage..." he was smiling as he went on, "...because that seems to be the right thing to do in a church. I don't believe you have to find a Bible text for everything in life, but you may be surprised to know that these scriptures have a lot to say about business."

Mark was curious but found himself thinking, "Right...this will be a stretch." Ken Jameson went on. "When Jesus was just 12 years old , we hear his first recorded words. In business terms, this was his first opportunity to make a pitch and tell us what he was about. He asked his parents a question: 'Didn't you know I must be about my Father's business?' Say what? Did Jesus just say business? I wonder where he got that notion from? Could it be that his time working in the family business is what prepared him for ministry? Let's take a look at an incident towards the end of Jesus' life on earth because it also involves a business. While you turn to the story in the book written by a medical practitioner named Dr. Luke, who was also quite the historian, I will mention this was not the first encounter Jesus had with a businessman. Apart from running his own business, a carpentry outfit, Jesus frequently engaged with business folks. Most of his followers were regular working people, not seminary graduates." He turned to look towards the pastor. "Sorry Pastor Mike, but statistically there is a better chance that if Jesus came to Silicon Valley today, he would come to my business not your church." People chuckled, and Mark wondered if this was true.

"Getting back to my favorite physician, Luke tells how Jesus told some of the disciples to head off into town and get things ready for a traditional Passover meal. He also said they would find a colt or donkey there that had never been ridden. He told these guys to go ahead and take the donkey. Hold on a second. Was Jesus advocating that they steal someone's donkey? And what did that donkey do? If Jesus was here today, what might the equivalent be?"

Ken had found the spot in his Bible and read a few verses to reinforce his point. "If anyone asks you, 'Why are you untying it?' tell him, 'The Lord needs it.'"

Teresa looked across at Mark. He seemed to be weighing what the speaker was saying with some intensity. Generally Mark was polite in regards to spiritual things; he agreed intellectually, but was not grabbed at a heart level. At work he operated more by logic than anything else.

"What was the donkey?" Ken was looking for a response from his audience. "Was it a pet? How many of you have donkeys in your living room? How many have colts tied up in the family room? My take is that this colt was probably an income earning asset, or income earning ass. It was part of someone's business. Or at least it was a mode of transportation, like a car today. So what I see here is Jesus sending a message to a business owner saying, 'I need your business.'"

Mark shifted in his seat and wondered, "Why would Jesus need someone's business?"

Ken began to tell a story. "I was down in Africa not so long ago and sat having coffee with a business owner who had a factory. I asked him, 'Charles, what would you do if your business was the only vehicle that Jesus had to reach the world?' Well, as we say in Silicon Valley, the screen saver went on...'" Ken motioned his hand past his face indicating Charles had a blank expression on his face. "'OK, Charles, forget about the world. How about sub-Saharan Africa. What if your business was the only shot that Jesus had of reaching a big chunk of Africa?' By now Charles was getting wise and he gave me the religious answer. 'Well, Ken, I would capitalize my business more, make more money, and then lay the money at the feet of those who do ministry.' That's what he said. How does that sound to you?"

Mark looked around and some people were nodding their heads in approval. "Generally when someone says they are going to make lots of money—do well—so that they can give it away—do good—they seldom get past the 'doing well' phase. So I usually don't buy that answer. But I knew Charles to be a man that had as a personal objective the goal of giving away 90% of what he earned. So I didn't think he was faking it. Nonetheless I looked at him and said, 'Charles, that's the wrong answer. You are not allowed to give the money away; you have to do the ministry through your business. What could you do?' Now I could see this was more of a stretch for Charles but we went into a dialogue about whether there was a market for his product in Africa, and how he could replicate what he does across 100 cities and towns in the target area."

"You might be wondering," Ken looked back to the Bible, "what this has to do with donkeys and Jesus. But Charles' factory is his donkey. I like how one translation states the instruction of Jesus: 'Tell them the Master needs it.' That same message is true today. God needs your business. Now you may be asking why this is the case. Let me outline several reasons, but before I do so I have to set the context by saying that God is in business. We have a crazy notion that working in this church or as a traditional missionary or social worker is 'ministry' but working in business is, well, just work. Nothing could be further from the truth. The Hebrews had, and still have, a word, *avodah,* which means two things: occupation and ministry. Somehow we have believed the lie that some work is just an occupation, but that there is a higher work, or vocation. The Germanic languages have a word for work, 'beroep,' which when translated means calling. Friends, business is a calling. All work is sacred, and God does not really value church work above accounting or marketing or engineering. My point to Charles: it is not his job just to make money and give it away to others who do good with his charitable giving. That would let Charles off the hook from figuring out some important questions, such as 'How am I conducting business? Are my business dealings ethical? How am I treating my employees? Am I using resources wisely? What is my environmental footprint? Would God be proud of my HR policies? Is my decision making by The Book? In short, how am I making the money?' Too often charitable organizations such as churches and mission organizations are happy to take checks from businesses without asking how the business makes money."

In recent years, Green Cycles had started to give more back to the community. As Mark thought about it, the initiative came from Whizz who was keen to see Green Cycles positioned as a good corporate citizen. Mark had no real intentions of doing anything "for God" with his charitable giving. But the speaker was right: it seemed people were happy to take his money regardless of how he made it.

"My point is not that we inspect every dime we receive to see if it was clean. What I am suggesting is businesses can themselves be vehicles for doing ministry. And, as I said, God has a business which is a little different from mine in that I deal with dollars and cents and payroll commitments and tax laws... but he does know business, and he told us to 'do business until I return.' Towards the end of his time on earth, he effectively said, 'If you don't understand the Master's business, you are not his friend.' I am sorry to tell you today, folks, that there are many Bible-believing people who have no clue about the Father's business, how he does it, and even less so, how he expects them to do business. According to John 15:15 they are not close friends with God."

Ken didn't seem to be trying to make people guilty; he looked like he was just reporting a sad fact. He went on to share stories of businesspeople from around the world who were finding out God is not against business, and that the Bible has lots to say about the topic. "I was talking with a man the other day who runs an advertising agency. I presumed this man was someone who believed in the teachings of Jesus but when I mentioned marketing principles in scripture he laughed. So I asked him, 'Why did you laugh?' to which he replied, 'I thought you mentioned marketing principles in the Bible... there are none!' He attended church regularly, had a degree from a good university, ran an ad agency, and did not believe that the Bible spoke at all to marketing. Friends, it is true that the word 'marketing' does not appear in most translations of the Bible.

But neither does the word 'missionary.' Yet you would agree that the principles of missions are inherent throughout scripture. Well, the same is true for marketing, product development, human resources, finance and all other facets of business. This," he raised his Bible in his hand, "is not just a Sunday School story book; it is a handbook for business, if we read it right."

Mark realized he knew precious little about the Bible, let alone what it said about business. While he was still not convinced Ken was totally legitimate, he did make some intriguing points.

"Before I tell you three reasons why God needs your business let me clarify one thing. The goal is not to get God into your business. The objective is to get your business into God's business. Jesus has little interest in becoming your ass keeper; he has every interest in your assets being put to work for him. You see, when they brought the colt to Jesus, the apostles took their cloaks and laid them over the donkey, and Jesus hopped on the animal and went straight back into the marketplace. Your business is supposed to carry Jesus into the marketplace, to work for him, to make him famous, to give him a better way to get into town. Who cares if businesses 'get religion' and are 20% more profitable if they don't actually get involved with what God is doing in the world? Not me."

"Way back when, God made a deal with a wealthy business guy who had set up shop on the trade routes between Cairo and Baghdad. The man had about 3,000 staff, a lot of assets, and by today's standards ran a pretty good sized operation. God said to him, 'Abie, I am going to make a deal with you: I will bless you and your business, and you will be a blessing to all nations.'

You may prefer this version from Genesis 12:

> The LORD had said to Abram, "Leave your country, your people and
> your father's household and go to the land I will show you."
> "I will make you into a great nation
> and I will bless you;
> I will make your name great,
> and you will be a blessing.

I will bless those who bless you,
and whoever curses you I will curse;
and all peoples on earth
will be blessed through you."
So Abram left, as the LORD had told him; and Lot went with him.
Abram was seventy-five years old when he set out from Haran.
He took his wife Sarai, his nephew Lot, all the possessions they
had accumulated and the people they had acquired in Haran, and
they set out for the land of Canaan, and they arrived there.

Abraham was doing fine, but God had a bigger purpose for his business.
You see, it wasn't about Abie, but about the nations, and God's business
involves having people from every nation become part of his operation.
So why would God need your business? Here are some quick thoughts.
First, the only sermon many people will ever hear will be the way you
do business. Do the math: most people go to work, not church. The
character, nature, ingenuity and brilliance of God should be evident in
everything from your products through to your profit. Second, the people
in your business are part of your household, just like Abraham, and God
intends business to be a way to bless employees, families of employees,
and customers. He also expects the business will be a positive influence
on suppliers, bankers...even lawyers!"

People chuckled when he mentioned lawyers but Ken interrupted them.
"Actually, I should not make fun of the legal profession because God is a
judge and I will appear before him one day. So will you. But I am relying on
my Advocate, Jesus, to make my case before the judge. How about you?"
Jameson snuck the lawyer story in quickly, but it niggled Mark.

He went back to his talk. "Third, your business can have access to any
country in the world provided you are offering a product people genuinely
need. I am not talking about using business as a front for missionary
activity; people see right through that. I am speaking of doing business
to bless people. Your business is a link to the nations." Ken paused to let
the words sink in. "That's why God needs your business. I will give you
three bonus points—three reasons why you need God in your business."

Teresa noticed Mark had reached for a pew pencil and was making a few notes. As Ken Jameson headed for his conclusion she saw her husband was attentive.

"So, why do you need God in your business? Reason #1: so you can discover your calling and live a life of purpose. The actuaries will tell you that you will work 66,000 hours, but if you do a startup or run your own business you know that the number is more like 80,000 hours, or more. Most people know God has a purpose for them, or at least they believe it in a vague sort of way. We should also know God expects us to work, just as he works. But they don't put two and two together and figure out that work is a calling. Taking two Greek words: 'occupacio' can be 'vocacio.'"

"The second reason you need God in your business is to give your business the right kind of purpose. Businesses with a clear purpose do better. But there is a difference between a clear purpose and a noble purpose. The better your purpose, the more likely it is your business will have a sustained impact. Why is this? The explanation is simple: businesses lacking purpose also lack alignment. When there is misalignment then there is inefficiency, and overall wear and tear on the company."

"The final reason why it would be good for you to have God in your business is a bit more subtle. If your business does not serve the one true God there is a distinct possibility you will make a god of your business and you will serve it. Let me speak personally. I might think, 'my business is a testimony to my brilliance and it reflects me,' but the truth is if I do not have God first, I will end up worshipping something else. We live in a pretty narcissistic culture where we, and I am talking about people of faith, have ourselves in the center—put an "i" in front of products and we are happy to buy them. So I need to make a clear invitation to God to be CEO of my business for my own good, to prevent it from becoming a detriment—to stop it becoming an idol."

"Let me wrap up by reminding you about the donkey. In many parts of the world today it would be a bicycle. What if Jesus were saying to you today, 'I need your bike. I need your business.'? What would you tell him?"

CHAPTER 16

Beyond Green

The rest of Sunday had been relatively routine. Mark thought Teresa would want to dig into what the preacher guy had said, but she seemed content just to let it be. Nonetheless, Mark found his thoughts going back to what Ken Jameson had talked about. A lot of it was pretty foreign to him. Religion belonged in its own bucket and he somehow figured there was probably something in the Bible about the separation of church and state. Or maybe it was in the Constitution. Either way, in California it seemed that one did better when one's religious beliefs did not get dragged into work situations.

"Work and private life should be separate." Mark said it to himself as he drove to work on Monday for the second week of Due Diligence. A question popped into his mind as he drove past a Google billboard. "If work and private life are separate, why are companies going to such lengths to make work more like home? Restaurants, fitness areas, day care... why are the lines blurring if these things are supposed to be separate?"

Mark's first meeting of the day was with Skylar and Raj to talk through the product portfolio. He anticipated being on fairly safe ground as he had a solid understanding of the product line.

"Morning, Raj. By the way, I forgot to ask how your ride went with the Green Team on Thursday?"

"It was a stretch," Raj admitted, "but I am still here." Raj spread his arms as if to present himself still in working order.

"Hello, Mark." Skylar was more businesslike. "Could you perhaps arrange a flip chart for our meeting?"

"Sure, I will have Tamara bring one up."

"While we wait, can you tell us more of the story behind your products, more of the history?"

Most company founders like to talk about their story, and Skylar found Mark to be no exception. The previous week's conversations had left her unconvinced Mark had either a clear purpose or a real passion. She hoped the product discussion would be more revealing. Mark liked to build things, and he liked to solve problems; that much was clear. But the first trait was common to people generally, and the second was especially common to men.

After Mark finished the story, Raj stood at the flip chart as he asked, "So, Mark, can you help me understand the key characteristics of a product that is 'green'?"

"Do you mean generally, or as it pertains to our business?"

"Let's talk generally first," Raj offered.

While Mark began to share Skylar listed the items on the flip chart. Mark noted that Raj seemed to be adapting to the Green Cycles dress code, but Skylar was back to last Monday's more business-like attire.

- The materials are recycled, or
- They can be recycled, and
- There are no harmful chemicals in the products, and
- The production process has low emissions, and
- The production process is friendly to people, and
- Waste is put to good use.

"That's very helpful, Mark. When we look at the green machines, which of these characteristics would you say most apply to your bicycles?" Skylar motioned for Mark to indicate his choices on the flip chart, so he moved over to where she was standing. She handed him a pen.

"Forty," he thought. "She has to be forty. Not that she looks forty, but she acts more than forty." He took the pen from her.

"There are over 80 components to a bicycle. In broad terms, the frame, wheel rubber, cabling... these items are definite. There are some specialized components that are cost-prohibitive for us to make ourselves, but we get these from reputable suppliers."

"Excellent. Now can you tell us the three or four major components of your bikes not on this list?"

Mark rattled off five or six items. They tended to be smaller in the grand scheme of things. "They constitute less than 15% of the bicycle, such as the handle bar tape, ferrules, and fairings, to name a few, and the cyclocomputer."

"By cost?" Raj asked.

"No, by mass," Mark clarified.

"And where do you source those?" Raj asked.

"It varies, but most of it comes from China, with some from Vietnam and India."

"And the primary raw materials are..." Skylar asked.

"Today frames are made of composites, the gearing and other items are stainless steel, there's a fair amount of aluminum, and the rest is pretty self explanatory."
"Mark, when you think about the affect of your products, are you hoping for a better environment or a better world?"

"I haven't thought about it... I guess ten years ago the environmental angle was unique, so I went with it."

"Is it still unique?"

"Yes and no. People are more aware of the environment, but the meaning of green has become blurred. Look on the coffee cup you are holding, Raj. What does it say?"

"This cup saves trees by using 10% post-consumer recycled fiber." Raj read the label, but it was clear from the expression on his face he was not sure what it means.

"How do you feel when you read the label?" Mark asked.

"At first I feel good," Raj said, "but when I look more closely at it I feel confused. I don't actually know what 'post-consumer' is, and I am wondering about the other 90%."

"That's exactly my point," said Mark. "Is that a 'green' paper cup? It depends on whether you focus on the 90% or the 10%, and what the negative footprint of the 90% is. So in some ways we have focused on the reduction of damage done, which is selling a negative."

"What's the impact of green awareness on Green Cycles?" Skylar had more to ask, "And are any of your competitors touting green?"

"To some extent every bicycle is green, because the alternative mode of transport is a diesel spewing bus. So our competitors, like us, push the healthy lifestyle aspects of cycling, but not the green component."

"Why not?"
"Partly because we already own the space, but mainly because it would eat into their margins. Our products cost more."

"So you are still focused on a better environment?"

"Actually, I think there is more to it than that, but I am not sure I can put a label on it."

"Let's say, for the moment, you were focused on a better world, what would it look like?"

"Are you talking about the whole world?" Mark's mind flashed back to the Sunday talk. "I don't see how I can impact the world."

"Okay. Let's talk about the people in your specific world. If you could list out everyone involved in some way in the production of your product, what would it look like?"

"Do you mean all my suppliers, and my employees?"

"Yes, and any sub-contractors."

"How far back do we go on this thing? What about my suppliers' suppliers?"

"We could look at those too."

"So at some point we go all the way back to someone working in a mine or on an oil field somewhere."

They began the process of listing the people affected by Green Cycles. Raj listed the groups of people, by category, in the middle of the page, and on the right hand side they listed the positive impact that Green might be having on them.

"Out of interest," Skylar was looking at the list, "what would a more holistic look at your products entail... what would be more encompassing than 'green'?"

"You can think about both the components, and the impact," Raj added.

"Well," Mark was thoughtful, "on the impact side we could look behind the environment to the health and well-being of our customers overall."

"What would that entail?" Raj looked genuinely interested.

"Our customer base could change. Instead of just the able-bodied outdoor enthusiast or sporting minded, we could think about anyone whose life could be improved by cycling."

"Such as..."

"Such as someone who cannot afford a vehicle... or someone who uses a bicycle for their work."

"And would you still keep the green theme?"

"Of course. We would have to retain this not only as a differentiator, but in order to not solve one problem by creating another."

"Good. What else?"

Mark paused. He was still thinking about the implications of getting a whole new customer base.

Raj stood up and joined Skylar and Mark around the flip chart. "Mark, how do you like my clothes?"

"I was thinking to myself when I came in, 'Raj is getting into the Green dress code pretty quickly'... no offense to you, Skylar."

Raj smiled. "Want to know something about my clothes? They are all slave free!"

"I have heard about that."

"I chose every item for today's meeting because each one has a story about the origin and production of the garment, from the cotton thread to the finished item."
"They don't look too bad," Mark smiled as he said this, "but what about the cost?"

"Immediate or long term?" Raj shot back.

"Both."

"In the short term, they cost a little more than what you get from the bulk, everyday stores, but they are less than designer labels."

"And long term?"

"The shirt and pants are made by previously unemployed people in India, and from 100% recycled cotton. They are important to me because of my roots. So I, for one, am prepared to pay more, not just for the story, but because I am building into the long term wellbeing of people in India."

"How about your shoes?" Mark asked.

"The shoes are more of a challenge," Skylar had strolled over, held out her hand, and Raj had obliged as he took his shoes off and handed one to her. "Generally there are three problems with shoes: the leather often uses harsh chemicals in the dye and this, in turn, pollutes water supplies. Turkey, for example, had challenges getting into the EU because of its water issues caused by the leather industry."

"I did not know that."

"The second problem is the soles. As you will know, there are often oil-based products in the soles of shoes, and these can have a negative environmental impact. Sometimes, however, it is just a challenge finding out what is in the products."

"What's the third challenge?" Mark was curious.

"The labor. As you may recall, major brand name manufacturers have had bad press in the US because of their factory conditions in China and elsewhere. Human rights groups are quick to complain, and corporations are quick to defend. Somewhere in the middle of the triangle between Western idealism, Capitalism and the need for job creation is a fair truth."

"If you go into a shoe store, or a coffee shop for that matter, and there is a label that says 'Fair Trade' it is about as complex to understand as the 'green' labels."

"Besides." Skylar chipped in, "when we read 'Fair Trade' we usually think about large companies not using their buying power to squeeze small producers. We seldom get into the full supply chain considering all of the issues."

"Let's get back to Green Cycles. I have pulled a rough list of the typical components in a mountain bike, and then broken them down into the related raw materials." Raj handed Mark and Skylar a sheet of paper with a table showing two columns: components and raw materials. There was a third column with nothing in it.

"One question to explore is where the raw materials come from, and how they are obtained."

"Can you explain more on the raw material production side?" Mark asked.

"Sure. We all have cell phones," Raj reached into his pocket and dropped a smart phone on the table. "Mine is brand A and yours is brand B. Both of them have Columbite-tantalite (Coltan, for short) in them, a product mined mainly in Australia, or in the Congo. If the Coltan comes from Congo, then child labor is a likely factor."

Skylar stepped into the conversation. "What's the likelihood that our favorite cell phone company ensures that they only use the Australia-sourced Coltan?

"Slim to none." Mark responded.

"By the way, do you see any Coltan in the typical bicycle?" Raj asked.

Mark scanned his eye down the list. Sure enough, the electronic monitoring components or cyclocomputer most likely have Coltan in them since it has a GPS component.

"Let's dig into the rest of the elements. Aluminum, titanium, plastic, rubber, oil, steel, glass..."

They spent time filling in as many items as they could on Raj's table.

"What do we do next?" Mark asked.

"I would like you to have someone in either R&D or Purchasing look at our rough list, and come back to us with a quick analysis of the possible and likely sources of materials of our Green Cycle components." Raj handed a clean list to Mark. "They should feel free to remove any components where my generic analysis is incorrect, and add others unique to Green. In fact, it would be helpful if they indicated where Green was different from other manufacturers."

"Let's take a half hour break before we shift gears. Mark, perhaps you can think about who can do that analysis with Raj, and I will prepare for our next session on Positioning." Skylar and Raj walked out of Mark's office giving him a moment to reflect, check a few emails, and decide who would be best on the sourcing homework. Mark thought Kim in R&D would be the best person to work with Raj. She had a background in Engineering but had a strong financial bent, and she could probably keep up with Raj. A few minutes later Raj came back and Mark walked him over to meet Kim.

CHAPTER 17

Green To The Core

Skylar came back into Mark's office a half hour later.

"Been catching up on emails?" Mark asked.

"No, I have been chatting with some of your folks in the coffee room." She smiled as if she had learned something he didn't know. "It is interesting to hear their thoughts on your positioning."

"Our positioning? What did they say?"

"Well, it wasn't a formal exercise, more just probing for perceptions..." It was clear she wasn't about to reveal what they said. Instead she moved them to the next topic. Mark noticed she made more of an attempt to be amiable when Raj was not around.

"There's another exercise we need to do related to your products, Mark." Skylar, back at the flip chart, turned a page and started drawing a square. "You will remember the typical four quadrant analysis used to understand product differentiation." Mark nodded his head so she continued. "There is a strong connection between your products and your positioning vis-a-vis competitors. Given our discussion this morning, what labels could go on the axes here at Green Cycles?"

Mark spoke slowly, clearly running multiple thought processes in the background while he began. "Hmmm, in the past I might have said Innovation and Green. But perhaps that should be changed."

"What would cause it to change?" she asked. "Could it be your changing competitive landscape with others catching onto the green theme?"

"That's one scenario," Mark said.

"And the other one?" Skylar raised her eyebrows, crinkling her forehead.

"Well, the other one depends on what we really want to accomplish. Is green enough? Or is there more? Our conversations over the last week, plus some other stuff I heard, makes me suspect there is more."

"Are you speaking of purpose?"

"Probably. So far our product differentiation has been linked to an environmental purpose and we have attracted a niche following because of it. That purpose fueled innovation for a while, but the realities of growing a bigger business and seeking efficiencies and adding different personalities seem to have blurred the simple focus we had 10 years ago."

"So you don't have one purpose?"

"Well, as you saw last week, even if we have rough agreement on a 'green' purpose, it means different things to Kris and Whizz, for starters."

"And you?"

"I am not sure what it means to me right now. Green, is still a passion, but perhaps a better type of company, or something bigger, like this..." Mark motioned to the flip chart as he left his sentence unfinished.

"Tell me about the Green customer base, Mark."

"As you heard in our short history, the key to our success was a group of people in the Pacific Northwest who latched onto our vision and then spread our story virally in the cycling community. They made the green machine concept cool."

"Similar to the Apple user groups in the early days, when it was still Apple Computer," Skylar offered.

"Well, our following is not quite as avid as theirs, but there are similarities and differences. Our customers believe in us and feel connected to our success—so that aspect is similar."

"And the differences?"

"We don't have sub-groups creating sub-products like the early Macintosh User Group out of Berkeley."

"But do you have product suggestions coming back from your community?"

"Whizz tells me some from time to time. He has online forums where he interacts with the Green community, although I am not sure how much of it is general environmental chit chat, and how much is specific to us."

"Can we ask him?" Skylar looked like she was suggesting something fun.

"Sure," Mark replied.

"Give him a call and ask him to join us."

Mark went to his phone to call Whizz.

"What's up?"

"Got a second?"

"Sure."

"Come over to my office. I am meeting with Skylar and we could use your input."

"Who?" Whizz asked, and Mark was glad he was not on speaker phone. Mark paused and said nothing... "Okay, okay" said Whizz, as if he had just remembered, "I will be right over."

Whizz bounced into the office, more than walked. He was wearing baggy shorts which contrasted the tighter black stretch knit shirt with the Nike swish. He had heavy short sox that looked like they would be good for hiking, and trail shoes. Clearly he was not worried about the Due Diligence process or making a corporate impression. Skylar shook his hand as he came in and noticed he was not the high touch type. As he pulled up a chair she said, "We can use your help, Whizz. We have spent some time talking about Green's products this morning, and were just getting into a discussion about the customer base."

"The Green community?"

"Yes, I don't really know how much of a community they are, how you interact with them, and so on. Can you bring me up to speed?"

"Sure. The way I think about it is this: there are those people who have heard about green concepts, and they are drawn to it, but there are those who see green. They believe it, live it, feel it. They get why we are different, and they are avid supporters... enthusiasts."

"Can you segment these groups?"

"I see them in three layers. Imagine you are slicing through a plant, for example. There are some that are green on the outside, but white, green or hollow on the inside. Then there others that, no matter how deep you slice them, they are green through and through."

"What percentages are green through and through?"

"In our case, about 35%, which is pretty high."

"And the rest?"

"Well, there are those who want to be green—they have good intentions but they don't know as much as the green core people. They are the middle layer. I would say there are about 40-50% of those."

"Which leaves us with ..."

"There are about 15% who want to look green. They like the cool factor, but they are not green at the core. They could be swayed to go another direction because of some fad or another."

"Such as...?"

"A lighter bike, or a new composite material that is trendy, but not good for the environment. Anything that's different. They are green because green is different, not because it's right."

"Are the core people the ones you connect with online?" Mark asked.

"Actually, we connect with everyone online, but in different ways," Whizz explained. "There's a general Facebook group for anyone who buys our product..."

"Right," Mark said, recalling the invitations.

"But the serious people are part of a more closed internal group. They have to be invited by another core green person in order to be able to join."

"And what do you do with these people that is different from your dealings with the others?" Skylar asked.

"Well, I run advertising ideas past them. I share early interesting articles, and I give them a chance to share their stories. They are extended family."

"Are any competitors part of this group?" Skylar asked.

"I hadn't thought of that," Whizz seemed momentarily taken aback. "But what if they are? Is there a competition for making the environment better?

So what if others get provoked to take care of the environment better?" Skylar was watching Mark to gauge his reaction. He looked mildly perturbed but tried not to show he was concerned Whizz might be squandering Green's competitive advantage.

Mark finally spoke, "How much do these people know about us?"

"Actually, I see it differently," Whizz looked pretty confident as he interacted with Mark. "The real question is, 'How much do we know about them?' I know how often they cycle, I know what they eat on the road, I know the vitamins they take, I know how many miles they cycle, and for lots of them I even know their heart rate!"

"How does that factor into your products? Is there a connection between their life habits and the bikes you design?"

"Maybe, maybe not. I certainly share feedback with our design teams. One example is building heart rate monitors into handle bars, like you see on exercise equipment. At other times we simply recommend complementor products like GPS systems for tracking their routes, etc.. But the products themselves are not my main concern."

"What is your main concern?" Skylar asked.

"Well, in speaking with hundreds of Green-ers, as I call them, they buy our story because they trust us. They do not have the technical knowledge to second guess whether our products are, in fact, green. So they have to look at who we are as a company, how we behave, and how we interact with them. Trust is key. So I am open with them, and they are open with me. If we have a faulty component, they cut us some slack and give us meaningful feedback because they know we are pushing the edge on things."

"So would you say your customers buy your bicycles because they are green..." Skylar raised her eyebrows and opened her hands to indicate that her question was open ended.
"That might have been the case many years ago, Skylar, but it has morphed since then. Now the green-to-the-core people buy our products

because they believe they are part of making a better world. Everyone wants to make a difference, and we provide them the opportunity to combine their passion for cycling and the outdoors with the chance to make a difference."

Skylar was impressed. Maybe she had judged too quickly and Whizz was more than just a graphics/biker enthusiast. Whizz interrupted her thinking.

"Customers have been taught even their buying choices can help make the difference nowadays. In the old days a few people got to make a difference. In today's world we can all make a difference in small ways, every day. In the more affluent parts of the world we can do this by choosing to spend our money in the right ways. For me and many others, spending clean is spending right."

Skylar shifted over to the flip chart. She drew three 4-quadrant charts on a single page. "Whizz, one view of the company is that Green Cycles is different from others because of two things: innovation and green. How do you see it?"

"Well, I don't see a difference between innovation and green, as you put it. Our innovations are pretty much green innovations. So I would lump those together anyway."

"What would you see, then?"

"Probably our Community on one axis, and our Cause on the other. I realize that the two are pretty much connected, but the products we sell are reflective of the cause we believe in. And the 'we' is not just people inside the company, but especially those outside the company who have jumped on our bandwagon and given us a critical mass of..." he was struggling for a word, but did not seem to want say 'customers.' "You see," Whizz went on, "they are not really just customers. They are people who are champions of a common cause. They are our outside representatives. They are community putting our raison d'être, literally where the rubber meets the road."

"I wonder how Kris would see this," Skylar found herself speaking the question out loud.

"Let's call him!"

Skylar and Whizz engaged in light conversation while Mark convinced Kris to stop in for 10 minutes. He came quickly, obviously not happy to be left out of a key meeting.

"Hi, Kris." Skylar tried to warm him, "We have been having a pretty animated conversation, and wanted to get your perspective. Raj and I are exploring Green's differentiators as a company—what makes you unique. So far we have talked about two perspectives. I was interested to know how you see it."

"Well, from my perspective, hearing what you say, I think that the Community and the Cause are the same thing... one and the same." He moved his head from side to side as he finished his sentence, as if he had weighed the matter, and settled in his mind by the time his head stopped moving. "Looking at it, I think the 'innovation' and 'green' have also become one thing. So in the past I would probably say two things differentiated us: Green innovation and a Causeful Community, if there is such a phrase."

"There isn't," Whizz corrected his English, "but we know what you mean."

"What about today, Kris—how do you see it today? What's changed?" Mark was the one probing for more.

"Well, as the only genuine non-American in the room," he cast a look at Whizz which said, 'you may look more non-American than me but you are really an American', "what's changed is we are the only manufacturer or assembler, at least, that is all-American. Ten years ago that was not a big deal, but since the US has lost so many manufacturing jobs to other countries, there is a growing desire to build locally. People appreciate that we do this."

"Do you really think it is a differentiator?"

"It is hard to tell. Product quality from overseas suppliers has really improved, and their costs over there are certainly lower. But I have a sense there are limits to how much globalization people will stomach. It's all well and good to think 'the world, global citizen' and so on, but when neighbors are losing jobs there is some value to being local."

"So the 'Think Globally—Act Locally' bumper sticker sums up your perspective." Mark said it in a way that tried not to sound like he had reduced Kris' thoughtful response to a slogan, but he was used to packing things simply.

"I think it is a little more sophisticated than that, Mark. It is more like 'Innovate for a better world, but implement for a better community or neighborhood or something.' I am not sure how to say it, but my main point is there has been a shift."

Raj came into the room as Kris was finishing.

"What did you find so far, Raj?" Skylar looked to Whizz and Kristoff and said, "Raj has been doing some homework with your R&D folks to analyze the components of your bicycles."

"Hi Kris, Whizz – good to see you. The quick answer is this: The company is green, but it is not clean."

CHAPTER 18

Corporate Calling

"Let's do lunch."

Mark decided more time was needed to unpack the morning's discussions with Kris and Whizz. Besides, there were fresh questions in his mind since the Sunday talk about donkeys and bicycles and Raj's comment about "green but not clean." He did some of his best thinking out loud and he figured an informal setting would be a good way to bounce things around without others knowing he was being introspective.

The five of them strolled to a nearby eatery that was mostly California cuisine, if there is such a thing, with a mix of anything from salads to burgers. Mark let his guests order first. Skylar chose a salad, dressing on the side. Raj ordered a vegi-burger and Mark wondered whether he was Hindu. "Sprouts?" the server asked. "Excuse me?" Raj didn't understand what he asked. "Do you want sprouts on your burger?" Raj looked at the server to see if he was joking. He appeared to be serious, so Raj said, "Sure!" then shrugged his shoulders. "When in California…"

This made Mark wonder where the Due Diligence duo was from, but he decided to save this line of questioning for later. While they were waiting for their food Mark opened the conversation.

"Last Friday we tried to nail down our purpose, and we didn't get to a conclusion. Today we talked about what differentiates us and again we had three slightly different views. I am wondering whether this is completely fine—we just have three complementary angles. Or is it more like things have shifted, and maybe there's a bigger purpose out there that we don't see yet. What do you think?"

"Not so fast," Kris interrupted, "I want to go back to what Raj said about 'green and clean.'"

Raj took a sip of his mint-ginger ice tea before replying. "Kris, the definition of 'green' is pretty vague, wouldn't you agree?" Kris seemed to half-nod, half cock his head, so Raj continued. "There are other thoughts about what constitutes a good product, not just for the environment, but for society."

"You mean triple-bottom-line stuff," Kris concluded.

"Not exactly. That just looks at finances, environment and community, and often means one's immediate community. But there are more ways in which a product or company can have a positive or negative impact."

Raj brought Kris and Whizz up to speed on the earlier conversations and then shared his findings in regards to the sourcing of components in most bicycles. "Because you have relatively sophisticated components, you would think they would be free of child labor, slavery or graft. This may or may not be the case because of the tantalite in your bikes. My point is not to make this a hill to die on, but rather to consider the reach a company can have, and to explore some implicational thinking on the supply/manufacturing side, and on the customer side. All of this can be input for crafting the purpose of the company, and determining whether it has changed."

Skylar picked up from Raj. "There are also basic positives a company brings to a situation, such as job creation, building skills, providing a community away from home... all of these can be common to any good business. There are also negative things a corporation can avoid, such as corruption. Businesses can make a better world by championing a specific cause, for example, and by producing products essential to a healthy society."

"So how does that fit into our three divergent views of how we differentiate Green Cycles from competitors? Which of us is right?" Kris wanted to know the bottom line of their analysis.

"That would depend..."

"On our purpose?" Mark asked. Skylar nodded.

"I have heard it said that companies can have a calling, just as much as individuals can have a calling. What would you all say to that?" Mark shared the fresh insight that sprung up just the day before as if it had been in his bookshelf for some time.

"What do you mean?" Kris asked.

"Do you mean, like, something they are supposed to do for the world?" asked Whizz.

"That could be it," Mark said. The truth was, he didn't really know.

Skylar and Raj were quiet, watching the interchange.

Whizz pressed Mark for more specifics. "Okay, let's say companies can have a calling; if that is true, name three companies that serve a bigger purpose than just making money."

"That's easy," said Kris. "Volkswagen."

"VW? You're kidding, right?" Whizz was incredulous. "How so?"

"It is logical: 'volks' means people, and 'wagen' is like wagon, obviously, so the very name says it is an everyday, affordable vehicle made by the people, for the people."

"And did it positively impact people's lives?" Mark asked.

"Ja, ja... apart from a few minor air cooling problems." He was smiling.

"Toyota. Same thing, but without the overheating and expensive maintenance," Whizz said it with a certain amount of smugness.

"Guys, guys... none of that would have happened without Henry."

"Oh, come on. Always has to be an American first. Us Germans were building things before you were even a nation."

"Caterpillar. They invented machines that changed the way we farm and build." Mark gave a second example.

"Edison Electric." Whizz added.

"Was it the individual who had a calling, or the company?"

"Does it matter? Thomas Edison didn't invent light bulbs on his own any more than I 'invented' green cycles on my own." Mark replied.

"Healthcare," Skylar dropped into the conversation, "how about the healthcare arena?"

"I would say Genentech has a calling to discover or create drugs addressing cancer. I have a friend who works there," Whizz motioned towards the North with his knife as he spoke, "and he would pretty much say it is a company calling,"

"Cardica... the guys doing the heart bypass gadget. I heard their founder pretty much went after that problem because heart disease was the #1 killer, and he had the calling to do something about it." Mark had met a guy at a party who told him about how his skills could be used to address a need God cared about, or something like that.

Mark looked at Raj and Skylar and asked them, "What about you: do you think a company could have a calling?"

Raj and Skylar looked at each other as if they were debating whether to share an opinion. After a pause she was the first to respond. "Let's look at the two ends of the spectrum first. You have already argued an individual can have a calling, and I agree. At the other end, I think a nation can also have a calling. It can exist to accomplish a particular purpose unique to its attributes and history. One could say the United States, a relatively young nation as Kris points out, has had a calling to discover and champion democracy. Each nation, just like each individual, brings something different to the table of humankind."

"But calling can be abused," Kris said, "and it can be handled in a heavy handed way, as recent world events will attest."

"I totally agree. Calling, like purpose, can be perverted, or more commonly, simply squandered. But it doesn't change the fact that people and nations can have a calling."

"I buy that..." Whizz concurred.

"If what you say is true, then it stands to reason families, or households and companies, can have a calling too, because a company is really a collection of people who are a subset of a nation."

"So that's a 'yes'?" asked Mark.

"The same is true at a city level," Raj chipped in. "Within a country there are cities that know their identity, and some that are floundering. They all collect taxes and spend money, but those who know their purpose have a much stronger focus."

"You also think this is true of businesses?" Kris wanted to double-check.

"The are many corporations started by good people with a noble intent, either in what they did, or in the way they did it, and today some of them have lost their way; their original mandate has been lost in the sands of history." Skylar looked like she would share more if asked.
"For example?"

"Coca-Cola, founded by a church-going Methodist, Asa Candler. JC Penney department stores, built on the Golden Rule. Quaker Oats was founded by Quakers, as was Cadbury's and a few other chocolate companies. By the way, did you know that slavery is a huge factor in the chocolate industry today?" Skylar asked. Looking around the table, no one seemed to know.

"One of my favorites is a company over 250 years old that made a huge difference to its host city and, by all accounts, the nation. Before I tell you its name I should say that it was started at a time when alcoholism was rampant; gin and whiskey were destroying society. A God-fearing man, who was also an entrepreneur, decided to fight fire with fire. His name was Arthur Guinness."

"The beer? How can beer be an antidote to alcoholism?"

"Well, he got the notion to focus on brewing Porter, beer with a relatively low alcohol content, and a high nutritional value." Raj explained. "Later it became known as Guinness Stout."

Skylar added, "The idea, so the legend goes, was for people to get full before they got drunk."

Raj picked up the conversation. "There are some companies that have kept to their calling, such as Service Master and Correct Craft, the guys who make power boats. They nearly lost the business when they refused to pay bribes."

"Many of these people sound religious," Kris said, "is that the case?"

"Not always," Raj said.

Skylar could tell Kris was both inquisitive, and a little defensive. So she thought she would explore his line of inquiry. "Kris, let's just say, to explore the religion route, there is indeed a God who is creative... for the sake of building a line of logic."

"Go on."

"And let's assume this creative God would have made man to reflect some of his attributes. So man, in turn, would be creative, and would therefore like to build things."

"I follow what you are saying."

"Let's just say God made the world, but didn't place on the earth, from the get-go, every product in its final form. Sand, but not silicon; oil in the ground, but not refined gasoline, or corn but not biodiesel. How would God actually get the products for which he had made inherent provision to market?"

"He wouldn't. Man would do it." Kris gave a true, but standard humanistic answer.

"You could be right and wrong. Could it not also be true he intended to do it in partnership with man?"

"What makes you say that?" Mark joined the conversation. "Didn't God just set everything up, wind the clock, and then let it tick on without much help? Why would he need man?"

"Partly my assumptions: remember I said that we should assume God is there, he is the Creator, and he made man to be creative. The other part is God has delegated certain collaborative responsibilities to man from the outset."

"Such as...?"

"Such as naming the animals. God made them, Adam named them. But it went beyond that. God was, according to the Genesis account, careful not to put certain things in place until there were men and women to manage the resources."

"So if God is pro-production and he designed things in a way that requires man's involvement," Kris was extending out the logic, "then you would say God is pro-business."

"Yes, given my assumptions, God would be pro-work, and corporations are there to organize work so that it happens better, so he would be pro-business."

Kris objected. "But many businesses take this productive ability and turn it towards bad purposes, such as making destructive products, or ripping people off in casinos."

"Is it not possible God has to take a risk that businesses, just like people, will go after the wrong purpose?" Raj asked.

"Or just act to limit their liability," Whizz interjected.

"In the old family businesses the limitation of liability was far from people's minds. If a family member messed up it affected everyone's reputation. It didn't help to say, 'But we have a Limited Liability Corporation.'" Raj said. "In fact, in many parts of the world this is still the case today."

"So, back to my question," Kris was curious, "are all well intentioned businesses started by religious people?"

"Not at all. Anyone who wants to do a good business for a good motive is, in effect, reflecting something of the nature of God, whether they believe in God or not. I believe it goes further. I suspect, and this is only my personal view, that there are plenty of products in God's mind that he wants to get to market, and if those who claim to know him won't work with him, he will give the ideas and passion to someone else."

"Why would he do that?"

"Let's say a father had three children. As young kids they were all creative, drawing him pictures and making things from rocks and sticks. They grew up to be inventive individuals who all started businesses making products of high value and good quality. Would he be proud of them?"

"I think he would," said Whizz.

"But what if one of them was estranged from him: how would he feel about that child's products?"

"I don't think he would think any less of them... I wouldn't." Whizz was emphatic.

"And what if he himself had a product idea he wanted one of the kids to run with; which one would he give it to?"

"I think the one that was most qualified," said Kris.

"So if the estranged son or daughter had the best qualifications the father might still give that sibling the idea to run with?"

"I would," said Kris.

"I think it would be the one who was closest to him," Whizz retorted.

"And I would guess the one who was closest to him would, in the long run, be more qualified," was Mark's response.

"Why would you say that?" Skylar asked.

"It's my experience creative people are stimulated by other creative people. So if the father was creative and one of the kids spent more time with him, then that person should be enriched by the experience. Over time, they become the best risk or option for the father."

"Go on."

"If God is interested in business—and that is still an *if* for me—then interacting with him should increase creativity, right?"
Raj looked at Kris and asked, "Do you remember the *Time Magazine* Man of the Millennium when we hit 2,000?"

"Of course, ja. It was a German, Guttenberg, because he invented the printing press."
"Correct. Have you ever read anything destructive in a book? Or have

you ever received a negative email?" People nodded. "Well, Guttenberg creatively used the technology of his day to print the Bible so that everyday Germans, like Kris here, could have access to the scriptures and read them for themselves. Until that time, only priests had the Bible. The potential for others to use the invention for destructive purposes did not, it seems, prevent Guttenberg from forging ahead with invention."

"Just like social media companies," Whizz added.

"Exactly," Raj went on, "Facebook or Twitter can spread good or foment evil...so the companies take steps to mitigate the downsides, but still stay in the game."

"Not to get too sidetracked," Skylar interjected, "but any company can start off with good intentions, and end up experiencing corporate drift. Even some of our favorite companies or institutions started off as corporations for a greater good, but as they grew beyond the founders the focus was diluted."

"Back to my earlier question," Mark did not want to lose this opportunity to settle some of his uncertainties, "do you think that it is fine for us to have different angles on the purpose of Green Cycles?" For the moment Mark had forgotten that Skylar and Raj were not part of the family, and he was being more vulnerable than perhaps he should have.

"For me," Kris stated matter of factly, "the bottom line is the bottom line. If we lose sight of that we will lose our way."

"That's not good enough for me," Whizz responded, "because if the bottom line is good and we make the planet worse in the process, then our business is not worth doing."

"Can't both of those things be measured and included in our purpose?" Mark asked. "And what about the people? If we have a profitable business and preserve the environment but sap the souls of people, is that good enough?"

"Which people?" Kris asked, probing for the scope of Mark's inquiry. He wasn't going to agree to something he saw as too vague or altruistic.

"Well, our stakeholders, starting with our employees," Mark clarified.

Kris was going for more specifics, and he knew Mark could be vague, and then assume everyone had agreed with his vagueness, so he would not let it go. "So our employees?"

"Yes."

"And their families?"

"Of course."

"What about our customers?"

"If we don't include our customers we will not survive," Whizz advocated.

"And our suppliers?"

"Well, that could be trickier because our relationships with them vary. Some are more like partners, and others are arms length," Mark expressed his perspective, "and I don't think we have influence with some guy we order stainless steel screws from online."

Whizz was nodding his agreement.

"So, if we can influence their lives then we have to take them into account?" Kris asked.
"As I think about it," Mark said, "if we influence their behavior to do something we would not do ourselves just so we can benefit, then we have crossed a line."

"Do we do this, in your opinion?" Kris asked.

"I am not really sure, simply because I have not examined it in detail. But this morning we began a conversation that might help us answer this question...this is the green versus clean discussion."

"How did we get to this expansion of thinking?" Kris looked perplexed, "Did I miss a meeting where you discussed this?"

"Not at all," Mark was assuring, "I think it is just a natural evolution and we have to take time to talk about it. When my kids were babies, I could pay for baby food and diapers and interact a little, and that was fine. As teenagers they have different needs, and I have different responsibilities. At the core, I am still a parent, but things have changed."

"So would you say Green Cycles has become a teenager?" Raj asked.

"As I think about it," Mark wasn't posturing, "I think Green Cycles is a teenager."

"So we are having a little teenage identity crisis?" Whizz asked. "Is that why you hired these guys?" He smiled as he said it so that Raj and Skylar did not feel awkward, but he was probing to know a bit more about their role. So far it had seemed pretty high level to him, and he wasn't sure where they were heading with the analysis.

Raj decided to bail Mark out by addressing Whizz's question.

"Whizz, when one thinks about the impact of a company there are a combination of factors either increasing or decreasing that impact. You saw in our 10-P analysis how we look at 10 such drivers. So far we have looked at Purpose, but we have also explored other areas, at least at a high level. We discussed your Positioning this morning, and last week Skylar touched on Process with Kris, and Presence with you."

"When Skylar visited my office?" Whizz asked.

"Yes, she learned lots about your approach to marketing and public relations...these spring partly from your identity and partly from your core beliefs or view of life," Raj responded.

"Then today we began to explore the boundaries of your 'household' or sphere of influence. You yourselves started to sketch the outlines of just how far that reach is, although we don't think you are settled on it yet."

"But you keep getting back to this Purpose thing..." Kris was asking, more than objecting.

"If your purpose is not clear and still relevant for where the company is today— right now—then it is hard to know whether your product portfolio, or your pricing, or your marketing, or anything else, for that matter, is on target." Skylar made the statement as if it was totally logical, and pulled her shoulders up and the corners of her mouth down to form a shrug that was more like a parentheses on the unsaid sentence, "And if we don't know your purpose, we don't know anything."

"Got it." Kris made the statement as he stood and pushed back his chair.

"Shall we?" he asked, indicating lunch was over and it was time to head back to Green Cycles.

CHAPTER 19

The Bombshell

Mark was beginning to think he was in over his head with the Due Diligence exploration. He thought it would be simple: get a valuation on the company, find a willing buyer, and either sell it, or keep it. If he didn't sell then there would be no need for anyone to know about the experience. Instead he found himself dragged into discussions with Teresa, which was fine, but also Kris, Whizz and Vera. More questions were being raised than settled.

"Why do I feel unsettled?" Mark asked himself as he drove home in the late summer afternoon. He loved California. The sun was still a good distance above the Santa Cruz coastal range and he decided to get home a little early and cycle into the mountains to hopefully clear his head. It would be relatively cool on the shadowed side of the hills. "How do I know which answers are right and which are wrong?" Mark got home, changed, and handed Teresa his planned route before leaving the house. Pretty soon he was out of Saratoga and onto the Big Basin Highway. On a relatively steep climb he was in the cool of the redwoods, or Sequoia trees.

"What's bothering me?" Mark asked as he pumped his way up the hill. It wasn't the due diligence process; Skylar and Raj had been polite and non-invasive. It wasn't his interactions with Teresa because he felt they had enough common ground. It wasn't even the conversation with Vera, although she was still an obstacle to a sale. Suddenly it hit him.

A Journey to Purpose

"I feel at a disadvantage with Whizz and Kris when we are having these discussions! Why is that?"

He had grown to know Whizz and Kris well. Whizz was likeable, warm and spontaneous. Kris was sometimes gruff, usually direct, and generally no frills. He liked them both, and valued what each of them brought to the table. He saw himself as the synthesizer of varying viewpoints, choosing a middle road, keeping them both happy. It wasn't hard to guess where they would be coming from on an issue. If he wanted to do something new, he would ask Whizz's advice to gauge how the Green Cycles community would view it. Then he went to Kris who would give him the pragmatic, "here's how it really is" opinion. There was a happy tension between Whizz and Kris, and Mark was the one who kept them both engaged, seeing each other's perspective.

What was becoming clearer from this last week's discussions is they did not really know his perspective, and worse, neither did he. So when it got to discussions on Purpose or Positioning it was Whizz and Kris' contrasting, but clear, opinions. "I just don't have the same grid, the same clear framework each of them uses, pretty predictably, to look at every situation." Cycling home he felt a bit better. At least he knew what the problem was.

He freewheeled into the driveway, checked his Garman Cycle Computer, and took it inside to load his route onto his laptop. It would give him distance, hill ascent and descent, heart rate, and calories burned. He moved towards Teresa who was in the kitchen to give her a hug, but she backed away, as she usually did, from his sweaty embrace.

"Later," she said to him. He knew it wasn't a promise, just a command to stay away.

Mark seemed more chipper on his return than when he left. "You look happier," Teresa observed. "Had a good ride?"

"I had a great ride, and I found out what my problem is."
"You have a problem?"

"I do. But now I know I have one, I can fix it. So I am happy. I'm going to take a shower."

Mark had always been an optimist. It was one of the things that had attracted Teresa to him when they first met. He had, until recently, also been quite stable. He was by no means boring, but was constant enough that she felt free to go along with his random ideas because they generally fit within the Green Cycles box, and at the end of the day, they seemed to work. This latest escapade, however, had threatened to get rid of the box, and that concerned her.

Mark bounced back into the kitchen twenty minutes later. "What's for dinner?"

"The kids are having spaghetti."

"What about us?"

"We..." she gave him a good smile to make it sound less ominous, "are going out for dinner. I made reservations in downtown Los Gatos. Put on some long pants."

"Cool."

Teresa appended, "There has been a lot going on and I need time to catch up and process things."

"So this is not just a romantic dinner then?" It was a rhetorical question, but he was happy nonetheless. Mark was keen to process some things with Teresa and knew the smart thing to do was to let her get through her own questions first. She had a knack for crystallizing things and maybe her course of discovery would clarify some of his thinking.

About an hour later they were sitting across the table from each other at an Italian restaurant. Mark appreciated the fact that Teresa took the time to make herself look good, not that she wasn't good to look at from the outset, but she had matched her earrings, blouse and jacket and necklace—he was going top to bottom—with thought and style.

A Journey to Purpose

"Thanks," he said to her.

"For what?" she gave a quizzical smile.

"For making the effort... the effort to look nice, the effort to set up the meal... the efforts at home. Thanks. I know you don't get a formal performance appraisal like people do at the office, so there you go! Good job."

Teresa looked at Mark. He had become better at verbal affirmation. She didn't diminish the compliment by deflecting it. "Thanks for noticing."

"Mark, what is happening at work? Bring me up to speed."

"You don't want to talk about your stuff first?" Mark knew that Teresa was a good listener. He also knew that in the past she had sometimes asked him a question, and he had waxed on for ages, when she really wanted him to ask her a question.

"No, I really just want to get caught up on where things are and how they are progressing."

"Teresa, it has been a little weird, but I think I have put my finger on something. Every time we have a conversation with Whizz and Kris..."

"Who's we?" she interrupted.

"Skylar and Raj and I... every time they talk with the three of us it seems predictable how Kris and Whizz will answer."

"Back up a little bit. What is new about this? You know them pretty well."

"I do know them well, but I did not realize they had such predictably different views on things."

"What has brought this into relief?"

"I think it is the discussions on purpose."

"How is that?"

"Well, Kris' answer to everything is pragmatic, logical, 'za bottom line'!" Mark faked a German accent. "So for Kris the purpose of the company is to make money and provide for the necessities of life, and everything gets evaluated against that plumb line."

Teresa nodded in agreement.

"It is different for Whizz. He sees everything through a green lens. If it isn't good for the environment, then it isn't good. He also has a grasp of our loyal, 'green to the core' customer base, and how they view things. He filters Kris's pragmatism through the thinking of the invisible green people he represents. It's not that he cannot see the bottom line, but he sees more of what drives the bottom line than Kris does."

"And this has been evident in your discussions this last week?"

"Absolutely. When we talked about positioning today, the differences were as clear as daylight."

"And what about you—what is your perspective?" She searched his face, genuinely wanting to know.

"That is the problem. Each of them has a clear grid through which they filter everything. Kris is the pragmatist, you could say humanist. And Whizz is the environmentalist. I know I have perspectives and things I believe, but they are a random collection of viewpoints on many aspects of the business that have not formed into a cohesive framework."

"How does that make you feel?"
"I feel at a disadvantage. Until now I did not need to have my viewpoint clearly articulated. As the final decision maker I would throw something out, get feedback from a variety of people, mix in a bit of my own 'whatever,' and make what I thought was the best decision. And it seemed to work.

I could be the mystery guy with the missing catalytic ingredient in the alchemy of things, and when I threw it in things got clarified, we made a decision, and we moved forward."

This sounded a little bit like vintage Mark, and Teresa wasn't sure others would see his logic and role as neatly wrapped together. So she asked him, "Do others see it the way you do?"

They had ordered food and were enjoying a pre-dinner glass of wine. He sipped his Syrah-Cabernet blend before responding. "Not really. Kris would like more logic and predictability, and Whizz would like more consistency in our 'green' stance. I think he sees me as not quite 'green to the core' and in danger of wandering from the wooded trail. He probably believes his informal job description is keeping me focused on the cause."

"What else?"

"I also feel I am in the cross-hairs. I thought this Due Diligence process would be about the company, about sales and cash flow and products, but instead I get the feeling we are stuck going forward until I know why I am in the business."

"Oh. Like the donkey guy said."

"The donkey guy? Oh, yes... the chap from the other day." Mark had been impacted by what Ken Jameson had said at the time, but the busyness at work had dimmed his memory.

"Yesterday," Teresa corrected him.

"It was only yesterday? You are right."

"I have been thinking, Mark, what if God does own our business?"
Mark stopped dead in his mental tracks. He knew that Teresa was further down the spiritual road than he was, but he never thought she would entertain the notion of God owning the business. He couldn't tell how serious she was, however, so he decided to not say, "You are

kidding, right!" and simply said, "...and?" which was one of those good joining words that let her keep talking and stopped him giving an opinion, something he had done all too often in the past.

"I mean, the bicycle-donkey analogy yesterday seemed to come at a time when I was asking for direction, so I have been wondering whether God has a claim to the business."

"Tell me more..."

"Let's say you owned a bicycle shop in Arizona or Texas and you had a manager running the store. What would you think if he decided to sell it?"

"I would be annoyed. I might even fire him."

"So, for sake of argument, if God owned Green Cycles and you decided to sell it without consulting him, he could fire you?"

"But he doesn't own Green Cycles, Teresa..."

She looked at him and inserted a "listen to what you just said" pause in the conversation to give him time to let his own words find their way back to his ears. He sounded a bit defensive.

"Shifting gears, Mark: the idea about God needing a business like Jesus needed the donkey—have you given any more thought to that?"

"Funny you should mention it, but it did come to mind today when we were discussing whether Green Cycles was having a positive or negative impact. I have always thought it was positive because we are better for the environment than other cycle manufacturers, and because we create jobs here in the US. But Raj did some digging today and some our suppliers could be using materials harvested using child labor."
"You are kidding."

"We are not sure, but we are looking into it. This has made me start to realize that Green Cycles has a much bigger footprint than I thought. In the past I just looked downstream to employees and customers. Today I had to think about a much broader group of stakeholders. So we could have a sphere of influence much larger than I thought."

"The child labor discussion prompted this?"

"It was more a lunchtime chat about what companies can do. If a business existed to touch people in some way, then God could have a significant reach through a company, just looking at the numbers. And if God truly owned every business run by people who say they follow him, then I suspect there could be a big ripple effect."

"What else came up today?"

"Back to my problem, I realized if I was not at Green Cycles then Kris and Whizz would try to take it in very different directions. So I get the sense that I have a key role to play there."

"And if we sold the company?"

"I think the new owner would pick a direction, cut out everything that is inconsistent with that direction, and try to get the company to make more money. One cannot fault them for that."

"Mark, what if we had not started the company? What if we were the ones buying a company someone else had started? How would we find out whether everything was being done the way we believed it should be done? Many of the processes and things that are in place at the company today are there because you and I, and even my mother, worked on them together. We had dreams and a philosophy of sorts, and these were part of the DNA...how would we know what to change in a company we acquired?"

"Are you trying to put yourself in Raj and Skylar's shoes?"

"Somewhat, but I am more asking myself, 'Teresa, what would it look like if you actively represented your 65% of the company?'"

Mark was stunned. "Sixty five percent?" he asked slowly.

"Yes, the 35% from our community of property, and the 30% from my folks. That's 65%."

Mark didn't know whether to be more shocked by the fact Teresa had done the percentage calculation, which he truthfully had never looked at that way, or the fact she was thinking about taking an active role in the business.

"Anyway," she ignored his un-composed countenance, "I have been thinking about what I actually believe about the foundational principles, as Raj called them, on which a business should be run."

Mark was still feeling a little flabbergasted, but she didn't seem to mind. She was getting on a roll talking about the things she thought were important in the company.

"I started with the people. In my mind they are the core part of any organization. How would people be managed in a company where God was the CEO, as Ken said? So I started listing things out: they would feel valued, they would all be growing as individuals, they would be encouraged to not sacrifice their families for the sake of the company, parents would be able to bring their kids to work and the kids would feel welcomed... stuff like that."

"What else?"

"I would get rid of the notion you cannot bring your problems from home to work. That is a stupid notion anyway. People are whole people and if they are struggling at home it will spill over at work. I think Jesus would have a work counselor, or something similar, who would speak with people and even pray with them if they had problems."

"That may be illegal."

"Whatever. I am just telling you what I would do if I were God and I owned the business."

Teresa was not finished. "I would try to make sure everyone in the company, from Tamara to Whizz, could make a connection between the work they did, the purpose of the company, and their own purpose."

"Teresa, don't you think that is a little idealistic?"

"If God owns a business I suspect things would be more than a little idealistic, don't you think?"

"I guess so." He was still taking in her 65% perspective and her new line of thinking.

"Besides, when I was speaking with Skylar after the purpose meeting last Friday—"

"You spoke with her afterwards?"

"Yes, she asked for my take on the meeting... Anyway, when we were chatting I reflected back on many of the conversations you and I have had, Mark, and it struck me that you are really trying to figure out your personal purpose. This whole experience with the sale of the company is just bringing it into relief."

Mark slowly motioned his head from side to side with a 'hmmm' expression on his face indicating that he may agree or disagree. "You really think it's about me?"

"It seems to me, based on what you have said tonight, Mark, that there are a number of things up in the air: your personal purpose, the purpose of the company, and how you and I make a determination about how to go forward. I cannot disengage and leave you to work through this on your own, if only because I represent the majority of the ownership. That's part of it."

"What's the other part?"

"The other part is I am your wife. We started this company together, and we cannot go through a major junction without being together. That's my instinct."

Mark, like most husbands, knew that "instinct" was code for "I have decided this and don't try to rationalize your way out of it." Mark wasn't sure he agreed with everything Teresa had concluded, but opted to save his ammunition for the days ahead, just in case he needed it.

"So much for romance," he mused. Mark had thought that the dinner would be more about Teresa dutifully drawing him out and helping him clarify his own thinking. Instead she had dropped a few bombs and taken him by surprise. He was genuinely shocked that she thought of herself as the majority owner of the company. On the other hand, he was impressed she had been thinking about which people principles were important to her.

The downside was it appeared the girls—Teresa and Skylar—were in dialogue, and it seemed the ladies had concurred he did not know his purpose. As if this was not enough, Teresa told him that she had cleared her schedule for the week and would sit in on many of the remaining Due Diligence meetings.

CHAPTER 20

Foundational Principles

The first thought in Mark's mind when he woke early the next morning was this: "Foundational Principles...Teresa is coming up with business principles!" He decided he needed to get a jump on documenting his own thoughts about how the company should be run. Mark knew himself well enough to know he needed to get on the offensive. He had identified a problem: he didn't have a clear mental map. Teresa had started formulating her own thinking, and Kris and Whizz had pretty set views. Even Vera was clearer about her take on the business than him. A month ago he felt he was in the driver's seat and today he felt he was under siege, or at least he had a tiger by the tail... or five tails. As he made a cup of Chai he thought, "There's the Skylar and Raj tail, the Kris tail, the Whizz tail, the Vera tail, and now there is even the Teresa tail!"

He headed to his den to think and write. Soon headings appeared at the top of yellow notepad pages. He needed to think less about processes and procedures, and more about the underlying foundations for each function of the business. Where to start... he decided to go for something concrete.

"I believe Green Cycles processes should be..." was his heading. Underneath it he began to list things that had become important to him over time.

- Open
- Documented
- Clear
- Transparent
- Constructive, not restrictive
- Predictable or consistent... make that, consistently applied, regardless of who is involved. (Is that "fair"?)
- Inclusive – we are a family and everyone cannot know everything, but we shouldn't lock out people under the guise of company policy
- Honest. It seems to go without saying, but given the discussion on "clean"...

He thought this was enough on process for now and flipped over the page. Mark tried to remember topics the Due Diligence team had raised to better anticipate their line of inquiry. He reached into his briefcase and pulled out the Impact Assessment spider diagram. "This is a lot of stuff..." he thought to himself. He picked another easy category.

"I believe Place should be..."
- Clean
- Fun
- Creative
- Welcoming
- Reflective of our care for the environment
- Autonomous—everyone can fix up their own space as they see fit, provided it does not negatively impact others
- Functional

Mark thought he was doing well with the low hanging fruit so picked another straightforward item.

"I believe Green Cycles Planning should be..."
- Done
- On time
- With the right people
- And a clear process
- With all assumptions on the table so that politics are minimized.

Mark decided to go for a more complex area, particularly given the discussions of the day before. Thinking about it, this could be an opportunity to minimize the collateral damage from Raj's research into their supply chain.

"I believe that in Partnering..."
- We have a responsibility to choose partners carefully
- We cannot control everything a partner does
- We can have influence on our partners, but not control (Is this too much like the prior point?)

"I believe our sphere of influence varies depending on ..."
- How much contact we have
- Whether we make payments to them
- Whether they are financially dependent on us
- Whether we impact their world (like our customers)
- How much we can influence the way they do business (maybe our suppliers).

Mark figured that this was a good start to Partnering and the sphere of influence concerns. He could always come back and refine things later. What did he believe about decision making? Was that a process item? He decided to list it separately.

"I believe decision making should be..."
- Transparent – no, I don't. Mark argued with himself as he made the list. That sounds good, but it doesn't work. "If I really believed in transparency then others would know I was selling the company."
- Inclusive – I don't believe that either. Not everyone can be involved in every decision.
- Fair – OK, I believe that.
- Consistent – well, that's the same as the process principle.
- Timely – yep, people should not be left hanging waiting for bureaucratic types to make decisions.
- Tested – actually, sometimes I think you have to go with your gut and you don't have time for testing.
- ...this area needs more work.

"I believe marketing ..."

- Should make people aware of genuine needs and not create fake needs (and then get people to throw good money away for things they don't need)
- Be consistent with the product being sold. (He and Teresa had agreed that they would not use good-looking women to sell cycling gloves, or other products for that matter. As far as possible, they used real customers to help market.)
- Should not promise what Green cannot deliver. (Have to check into the definition of "green" – has it changed, and are we true to this?)

Mark felt he had done all he could for one morning, made Teresa a cup of tea, and headed up to his room to get ready for work. He showered, dressed and joined the family for breakfast. He quite liked the early morning start and felt more ready to face the day. Justin was chatting about his upcoming camping trip. "Dad, do you think I can get some head lamps for my friends?"

"LED lamps? Sure... how much are you willing to pay?" Mark teased him. "How many do you need?"

"Six."

"Six? Holy moly... you will bankrupt the company. OK, I will sell them to you at cost."

"But I promised my friends I would get them."

"Be careful not to make promises next time before you check with your supplier." Justin looked a little forlorn. "Just kidding! I will get them for you. Send me a text later to remind me."

"Kelly, how are your projects going, sweetie?"

"Which ones?"

"The ones on the Internet... you know..." Mark had forgotten exactly which project she was doing.

"Dad, I do all my projects on the Internet... you know." Kelly was at that age.

"Honey, I will drive with you today." Mark's look gave away that he had forgotten that Teresa was coming to the office with him.

"Great!" he said as he regained composure.

They saw the kids off to school and while Teresa wrapped up a few items Mark began to go back over his list of beliefs or principles, he supposed one could call them. Since he was action oriented, he was not inclined to get everything down in writing. Reading them over, they looked more like the rambling sayings of Mark Green than a well thought through set of principles. He decided to enlist Teresa's help.

Driving to work Mark thanked Teresa for the dinner conversation. "It got me thinking about what I believed about the different facets of the business, and I made some rough notes this morning. While you were getting ready I scanned them again, and they are very rough. I didn't cover People because you already have that taken care of. I was wondering if we could spend a little time working on these between meetings."

Teresa dug in Mark's messenger bag and pulled out the yellow pad. He was still talking. "As I said last night, the other guys seem to have a clearer handle on what they believe..."

Teresa began reading Mark's notes from the morning. Some of it was good; some of the revisions were funny. "Sure...we can do it."

"You're not offended that I started making my own list... I was mimicking your list of People principles you shared at dinner."

"I am not offended at all. Can I give you an observation?"

"Go ahead."

"Some of these look really great, and some look like the sayings of Yogi Berra!"

"I know, I know... but we have to start somewhere." They laughed together. Mark enjoyed having her back in the morning work routine with him, albeit temporarily.

Their first meeting was with Skylar, Raj, Whizz and Kris. After the pleasantries Skylar began by outlining the schedule for the rest of the week. "First, let me begin by welcoming Teresa again. She will be joining us for most of the scheduled meetings this week. I am sure it is not necessary, but let me reiterate why I think her presence is essential. When Mark and Teresa began Green Cycles many years ago she was an integral part of the business. As such, her DNA is in many of the processes. She has not been involved for quite a while and I am keen to get her insights on whether or not the organization has drifted since those humble beginnings."

Skylar noticed Kris was bristling a little while she was speaking. Earlier interactions revealed he was not overly thrilled about Teresa's participation; perhaps he had aspirations about a greater role in the company. Skylar wondered if he felt threatened by Teresa, so decided to press a little and see. "The other factor, from a legal perspective, is that she is a major shareholder. Some would say a majority shareholder."

Mark looked at Teresa. Had she spoken with Skylar? He could tell from her face that she had not. Kris resigned more than reclined, and Skylar went on.

"Last week we had long conversations about your purpose and how this related to your positioning. Raj spent time on your supply chain and I have examined the Impact Assessment specifically in regards to production planning and manufacturing. We think you are running a good operation. On the marketing side—what we separate into Presence and Positioning—we have not yet settled the positioning, but it seems to contain three clear dimensions, namely, Cause/Customer, Green/Innovation, and Business Efficiency. Perhaps the normal quad analysis will not suffice and we will have to go 3-D. Your marketing is passion driven and builds off the strong relationship you have with your avid customers. They really are an asset. It is not, however, what we would call an integrated marketing strategy, but it nonetheless has some real high points. We were gratified to see that you have not resorted to the 'pretty girl sells shiny bicycle' advertising. That too is a tribute to a long standing policy which I believe was set in place by Teresa and Mark from the outset."

Mark thought, "Whizz must have told them about our early advertising decisions" and also mused that some of his own early morning reflections might be on target.

"There are a number of areas we have yet to explore, however, so this week we will focus on Partnering, Place and People. We will also get a deeper understanding of your Planning. Mark has outlined some of it, but we want to dig into the breadth of involvement from various stakeholders. That will leave us with some outstanding areas, and we will eventually get to Process and Profit. After all, the bottom line is sometimes the bottom line." Skylar smiled as she finished. "We have created a schedule of meetings which Tamara has placed on your Google calendar. You should all have the notifications. Are there any questions?"

The group talked, confirmed upcoming meetings and soon headed in different directions. Mark arranged for lunch to be brought in and blocked off a few hours with Teresa. She, meanwhile, left to attend a meeting with Raj, and he tackled some of his emails before going to a meeting with R&D.

He got back from the meeting and there was a note from Tamara on his keyboard. "Vera called. Ken Jameson can meet you tomorrow at 11 a.m."

"I did not ask for a meeting with Ken Jameson!" Mark said aloud. "Do I have a choice?" Vera had never interfered in their marriage, nor in his affairs. But last Saturday she seemed pretty adamant that Mark get this decision right. Evidently she had decided he needed some help.

Teresa came in at eleven and Mark dialed Tamara to order in some lunch. When he hung up he passed Tamara's note to Teresa and asked, "Did you know about this?"
"Not exactly."

"What does that mean?"

"Well, I did see mom corner him after the Sunday service but I have not spoken with her since then to find out what they talked about."

"Interesting. Well, I guess I could blow him off or meet with him."

Teresa did not respond and Mark pulled out his yellow pad with the morning musings. They agreed to go stream of consciousness on the various topics and jot down everything that had seemed to be important to them regarding the principles underlying the business. After a few hours they had quite a list and Teresa offered to bring some coherence to their musings. They agreed to sleep on the emerging notions, and take time for coffee on the way to work in the morning to refine them.

Mark occasionally encountered Skylar and Raj as they buzzed back and forth around the premises during the day. He had decided it was counter-productive to try and control their agenda so he gave them free rein. They seemed discrete during the first week, and even bailed him out once or twice when he was having trouble explaining what they were doing around the business.

Before he left for home he called Jameson's office and spoke with his personal assistant. "Edna Burrows, how can I help you?"

"Wow, that's an old fashioned name," Mark paused while he took it in. Fortunately he did not verbalize it but said, "Yes, Edna, this is Mark Green and I am calling to confirm an 11.00 a.m. with Ken Jameson tomorrow." Mark grimaced as he said it. He had been set up and he was already averse to the inevitable hour.

"Mr. Green, Mr. Jameson will be in your area and would like to meet you at Peet's Coffee on De Anza Boulevard. Do you need directions?"

"No thank you, Edna. I will be there."
The next morning Mark and Teresa decided to work from home for a few hours rather than go for coffee since he had the Jameson meeting at

eleven. He contemplated cancelling once or twice but figured there was no easy way around Vera. He would humor her, have the meeting, and be done with it.

Teresa had put in a serious effort pulling the collection of thoughts together. "Mark, this was a useful exercise for me."

"How so?"

"It made me recall some of the things we had on our hearts to do when we started the company. Looking back I think that in some cases we were dreaming, and in other cases we were on track. It has also made me realize we have drifted from the basics in a few areas. I know the business has become more complex, but I am not sure it justifies these shifts."

After they had discussed Teresa's concerns they delved into different areas and Teresa printed a fresh copy of their business principles for Mark. He kissed her on the cheek, pushing the notes into his messenger bag as he left for his meeting with Jameson.

Ken Jameson looked a little older at short range than he did from the pew on Sunday morning. Mark put him in his early fifties. He seemed in reasonable shape and had a twinkle in his eye that said, "I'm not as old as my body looks." After speaking with Edna Mark expected Jameson to be in a suit, but he sported a casual shirt and a lightweight jacket.

"Thanks for meeting," Jameson had arrived early and secured a table away from the barista action. He stood and extended his hand as Mark approached. Ken had a copy of Mark's bio at the table in front of him and obviously knew who to watch for. Mark glanced and it and Jameson explained: "Dame Edna." As they stood in line to order coffee Ken dove right in.

"Vera has given me a little context, and we can get into specifics in a moment, but why don't you tell me about yourself? Where you were born, where you grew up, your schooling..."
Mark hadn't known what to expect but there didn't seem to be any difference between Ken the preacher and Ken the business guy. He found

himself easily sharing his story. Ken had the ease of a father who was happy to see someone else succeed rather than the young buck angst of someone who still had something to prove. By the time they got back to the table Mark was telling Ken about the unease he had been feeling in recent years and how it led to him retaining a business broker.

"Where does your wife land on all of this?" Ken asked.

"I don't know yet. We have talked for a few years about my growing unrest, and she has been sympathetic. But she was shocked I had not consulted her before hiring the broker."

Ken laughed. "You didn't ask her first? Oh, brother. You're in trouble."

"Well, it hasn't been that bad. She has been good natured. Now she is involved and is taking it much more seriously than I imagined. Vera has also entered the fray and I got more than I expected from her."

"She summarized her ultimatum for me," Ken said. "And how are your colleagues at work taking it? A due diligence process can create a lot of churn."

"They don't know I am contemplating selling."

Ken was genuinely surprised. "Your management team doesn't know— how did that happen?"

Mark explained the series of events, giving Ken the headlines.

"So where does that leave you now?"

"Well, we seem stuck in several areas. The Due Diligence team is plowing forward but some things are inconclusive."
"What's the hold up?"
"It seems pretty clear to them that we don't know what our purpose is, beyond the basics of supplying a good product to happy customers and preserving the environment while making money."
"That sounds fairly reasonable to me," Ken affirmed.

"The challenge is our purpose sounds different when it is expressed by the two key managers and me. The buyers aren't trying to press us one way or another; they just want alignment. If we cannot agree on our purpose, then we cannot settle the positioning, and so on."

"Tell me about your two key managers."

Mark proceeded to share with Ken the brief history on Whizz and Kris, and how they each had differing, yet essential perspectives.

"I like these guys," said Ken, "but it is clear you have a clash of at least two worldviews."

"What's that?" Mark asked.

"It goes by different names, really, but one's worldview is a set of assumptions or preconceptions about the way the world works. Everyone has a worldview. Kris sounds like a good old humanist, and I would say Whizz could be a pantheist."

Mark wasn't really following, and he figured Ken probably knew it. "I am not sure I am following you."

"Let me put it this way: there are three major outlooks on life, each of which has a bunch of associated assumptions or lenses. When we look at a business problem, or anything in life for that matter, we tend to look through our chosen pair of spectacles. The first set says, 'There is no God, it is up to us to use our brains and make the most of things. Human effort can accomplish a lot of good.' Another view says words to the effect of, 'God is in everything and in all of us... so we need to look after everything and everyone as if god is in it all.' There are variations of the theme, but that's the gist of it."

"And the third group?" Mark realized that Ken had described Kris and Whizz's perspective on things without even meeting them. He wanted to know what else was in Ken's deck of cards.

"The third group: theists."

"Oh, you mean the Christians."

"Not necessarily. A theist simply says there is one god. So the Jews, Muslims and Christians all come from the theistic camp."

"But do they all agree on the same god?"

"It doesn't matter in this analysis. The label 'theist', as opposed to atheist, just refers to someone who believes in one god."

"So what you have as an underlying tension with Kris and Whizz is a differing worldview. And it will color many of your conversations."

Ken paused then asked Mark, "How about you? What is your worldview?"

"Umm, I would have to say I am a theist. I believe in a god."

"And how does that affect your conversations at work?"

Mark wasn't sure what Ken was asking. "Are you asking whether I talk about God at work?"

"Gosh, no," Ken seemed adamant this was not the case. "I am asking how your belief in one god informs your view of business. I am asking how your knowledge of God, assuming it is the so-called Christian God, translates into your practice of business."

Mark didn't look like he was about to answer, so Ken kept going. "You see, when you have to make a big decision Kris probably says, 'We have to be practical and think about the bottom line,' and Whizz says, 'We have to take care of our customers and the environment, and the bottom line will take care of itself.'"

"That is exactly what they say," Mark blurted out somewhat involuntarily.

"And what do you say, Mark?"

"Well, I am the middle of the road guy, the reconciler of their viewpoints."

"That's what you do, which is good, but what are your underlying assumptions. What is the grid through which Mark views the world?"

"It is interesting you should ask, Ken, because Teresa and I are working on that framework right now. Can I show you?" Mark did not wait for an answer and was already reaching into his bag like a man reaching for a lifeline in a storm. He put the freshly printed pages from Teresa between them on the table.

"For example…" Mark began to share the newly minted principles with Ken. Ken looked over the list and seemed to suck them in like an ATM taking in a debit card and verifying it against some hidden stash of information.

"I see you have organized it in ten areas; is that what the Due Diligence guys gave you?"

"Yes, it is."

"OK. We will work with that. Now tell me, since you are a theist, what does your god say about products and product development?"

Ken didn't appear to be trying to trip him up, so Mark attempted an answer. "That's a good question, Ken." Mark was stalling and looking at the list he and Teresa had compiled. "My feeling is that God wants products to be good for people, and to help them have a better quality of life."
"Good," said Ken, "that sounds great. And how do you generally involve God in the product development lifecycle?"

Before he could stop himself Mark asked, "God wants to be involved in the product development lifecycle?"
"Mark, if you owned a company, wouldn't you want to have some involvement in the products?"

"Yes, unless I had hired someone else to do it."

"Fair enough. Talk to me about your assumptions for Planning that you have listed here."

Mark walked through what he and Teresa had written down, and their rationale. Ken didn't comment that much but instead shifted focus as he turned over the paper to the blank side. "Explain to me how you typically make decisions, Mark."

"Sure. First, I get an idea..."

"When do you get most of your ideas?"

"When I am cycling."

Ken drew a picture of a bicycle. And next to it wrote, "Mark gets idea!"

"What happens next?"

"I chew on it for a while, and if it seems like it has legs I generally talk to Whizz about it."

Ken drew two more items: a set of teeth, and next to it, "Mark chews on it" and then a box with "Mark speaks to Whizz."

"Then, if Whizz buys into it I think about how to sell it to Kristoff, because he has a tighter filter than Whizz." Ken drew two more boxes: "Package for Kris" and "Speak to Kris."
"After that we either kill it, or do some more research, or decide to move forward. So it is pretty simple really."

"Mark, it looks straightforward, but I should add to the diagram that Whizz and Kris both apply filters to their decisions, and those filters are their worldview, right?"

"I see," Mark said, although had not thought to add those to the flow chart.

"Mark, may I be blunt with you because neither of us has much time?"

"Go ahead."

"I see very little influence of your worldview on your decision-making process. A person who sees the world through the lens of "one god" usually involves that god in decision-making, unless their god is impersonal and/or uncaring. Now I assume, and correct me if I am wrong, that since I met Vera in a church setting and she is your mother-in-law, that when you talk about "one god" you are actually referring to the One God of Hebrew and Christian writings… the One we could find in a church, among other places."

"That's a fair assumption," Mark said.

"There was a king of Israel, a long time ago, who agreed with his people it was essential to involve God in decision making. The book of Chronicles records for us that under King Asa the nation made a covenant 'seek the Lord with all their heart and soul.' That meant that they committed to involve him in their decisions, looking for his guidance. They went even further and agreed anyone who did not 'seek God' would be put to death."

"Wasn't that a little harsh?" Mark asked.

"Harsh or not, it was their attempt to make their worldview practical in one area, namely, decision making. I am not recommending it as your yardstick, but simply using it to highlight one of your most basic business processes—decision making—has no reference to or reliance on God."

"I see your point," Mark had to agree that Ken's logic was right, even though it was not his intent to keep God out in the cold.

"Mark, as I look at your list of principles here, they are mainly common sense and best practices. They don't show much sign of being infused with the ways of God or the thinking of God. In fact, if I were pressed to describe your worldview, it is the same as probably 90% of church-goers I meet."

"What is it?"

"It's a hybrid worldview: you are a Christian humanist."

A Journey to Purpose

"Meaning?"

"Meaning Jesus is your ticket to heaven, but he is not the CEO of your company. In regards to your salvation, you trust him completely, but when it comes to your business you trust your own training, experience or instinct."

Mark had no argument, except that it seemed Ken assumed Mark knew more about the Christian side than he did.

"Mark, I'll tell you what. I will meet with you once more, same time next week, provided you complete a homework assignment. You will have heard on Sunday that I don't require a Bible verse to validate every truth, but in your case I want you to find a scripture from anywhere in the Bible to support the views you and your wife have expressed on these pages. Will you do that?"

"I will do it," Mark found himself saying, although he had no clue about where to begin.

"Same time next week," Ken said as he stood, placed a hand on Mark's shoulder, and then walked out of Peet's.

Mark sat down again, somewhat stunned. "So I'm a Christian humanist, maybe without so much of the Christian part?" He had both hands on the table, the papers with the decision chart lay in between his hands. After a while he cleared his throat. "Hchmm. God, this is Mark here... from Green Cycles. I just want to set the record straight. I didn't mean to exclude you; I just didn't know you were that interested in business. That's it. Amen."

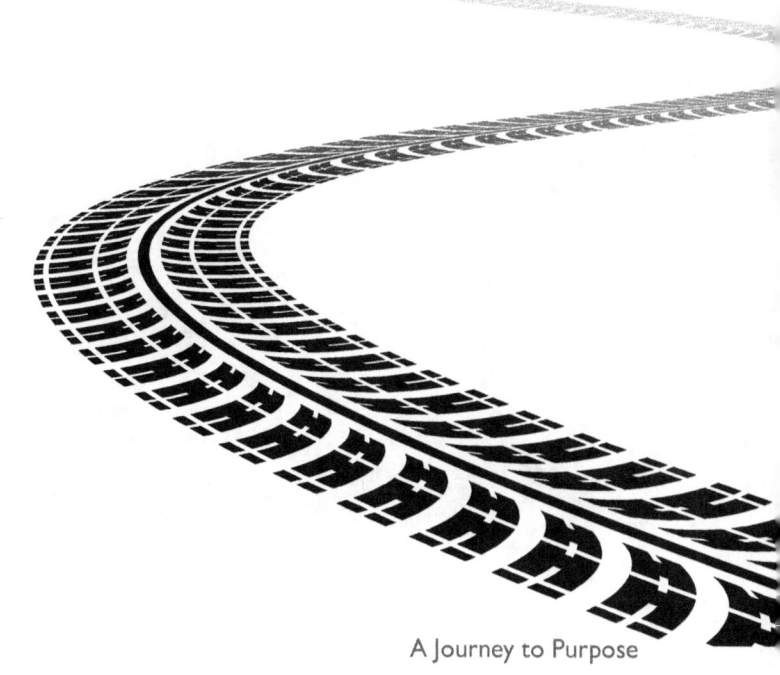

A Journey to Purpose

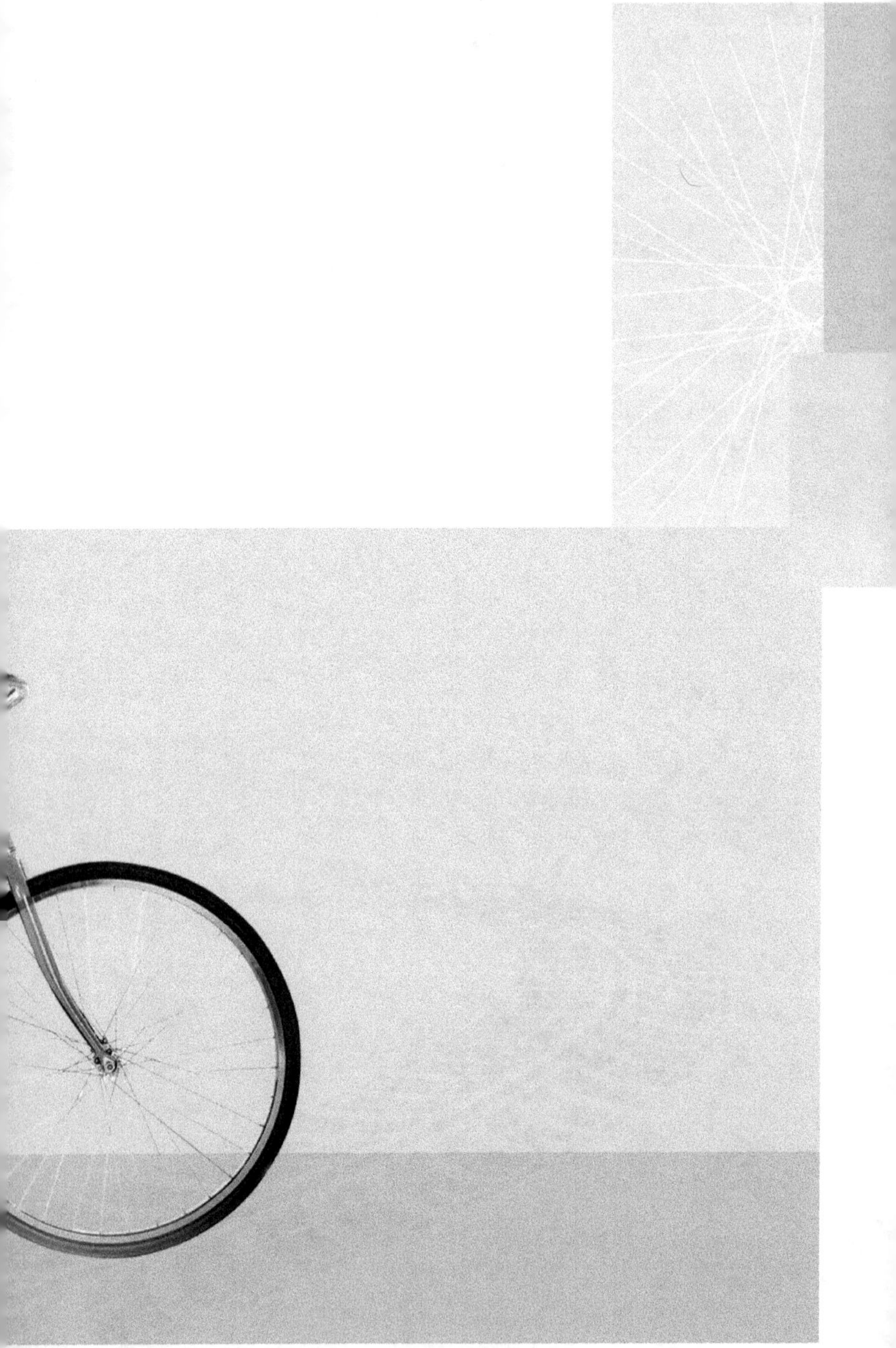

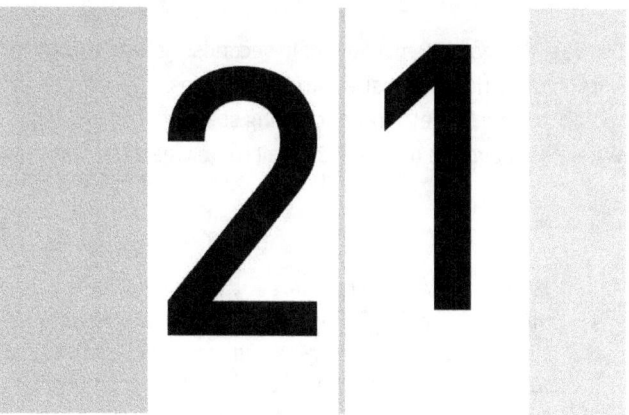

New Ownership

Mark spent a while longer sitting in the coffee shop. His encounter with Ken felt like a biology class, except he was the one being dissected, not some nameless frog. On the one hand he was relieved to know his suspicion was well founded concerning the grid, or worldview, of Whizz and Kris. On the other hand he was anxious about having no clue whatsoever regarding his own worldview. If it existed, it was half-baked. It seemed, with hindsight, he had brought his gifts and personality to bear on the business. Any Christian notions he harbored were not translated into business philosophies or practices. Was he supposed to do the God-in-business thing Ken talked about? If so, how? For Kris and Whizz, it seemed their actions flowed naturally from their identity. With him there was no direct connection.

When he got to the office he looked for Teresa to share what had transpired with Ken Jameson. She was in a meeting, so he scanned a few urgent matters, then took out his list of principles, wondering what Ken had in mind. "A scripture for every subject" was what he remembered him saying. Where was he going to begin? Google. What if he Googled "god + business"? It seemed to be worth a shot. Mark typed it into his browser and got 220 million hits in seconds. He was surprised; there were numerous articles, websites and references to books dealing with the topic. He felt a lot better about having something to show Ken next week. When Mark popped over to his email there was a new message:

> Mark,
>
> You seem like a pretty smart guy who could find a quick way around things, so I thought I would clarify the homework assignment. I just want one or two verses supporting your beliefs for each of the 10 areas you mentioned. I don't want someone else's views, just what you and your wife think is salient.
>
> Good meeting you.
>
> Ken
>
> PS: Forget Google—go to www.Biblegateway.com if you need some help.

"Who is this guy?" Mark wondered.

Mark clicked on the link. It was some sort of online Bible with a search capability. He picked an easy one: profit. Bingo, there were lots of hits in the Bible for profit. He copied and pasted them into a new document. "This ought to get me going," he thought as he tried the next one. "Planning" – nobody home. How about "plans"? Plenty of responses. Mark worked his way through the various areas, finding what he could, dropping them into a document, and printing them out to discuss with Teresa later. Some of the verses, at first glance, seemed pretty obscure. For other topics, like Product, there was nothing. Yet people seemed pretty convinced about God being involved in product development, so he would have to think about it.

He had a meeting scheduled with the Due Diligence Duo and Teresa at 2 p.m. There was a topic they wanted to introduce and get Mark's thoughts on. Skylar came into his office at about 1.45 p.m. She was early, and it looked like it was not an accident. Mark noted she was wearing the feather pin again and made a mental note to get Teresa to ask her about it.

"Hi, Mark."

"Skylar," he nodded as he said her name. "How are you today?" He sounded more poised than he really was.

"Great, thanks. I just had a good lunch chat with Teresa and she tells me the two of you are working on a Code of Business of some sort."

"Yes, she started it actually. We are trying to get down on paper the non-negotiables when it comes to the different facets of the business. We are using your 10 categories; hope you don't mind."

"Go right ahead. They can be useful sometimes."

"Anyway, we have a long way to go."

"Why, if I may ask, are you doing this... writing things down?"

"That's a good question. During our various meetings there have been all these questions about the company, and I realized why I felt bothered about some of our conversations."

"I noticed there were times when you were not fully engaged. What's been the challenge?"

"The dilemma, or trilemma, I suppose, is this issue of worldview..."

Skylar had not heard Mark use the phrase before, so she was curious. "And what's the problem with worldview?" she prompted for the rest of his thinking.

"Simply put, Kris and Whizz have one, and I don't."

"That's strange. I have always thought that everyone has a worldview. They just seem to have differing degrees of awareness."

"Right...that's what I am saying. Kris and Whizz act consistently with their worldview on a predictable basis, and I don't."

"You don't know what it is, or you know what it is and you don't act consistently with it?" Skylar knew the answer but wanted Mark to think about it some more. Just then Raj and Teresa arrived.

Raj and Skylar had concluded the challenge they were having with Mark was he did not have much foundation to build on when it came to the core issues of the business. He was fine with best practices and business basics, but he lacked an understanding of the deeper principles. Switching the focus of the meeting, Skylar transitioned to the topic of sustainability.

"Oh! Hi, Teresa. Good to see you. Hello, Raj." She let the conversation with Mark trail off. "Today we want to chat a little about a topic that may have some relevance to your business," Skylar continued. "Mark, when you think of the environment, how would you describe your responsibilities?"

"We have talked about that at Green Cycles. We want to pass on to the next generation a physical world that is better than the one we got from our parents."

"Why do you want to do that?"

"The earth is bigger than any of us, and it exists for the benefit of more than any one person. At the same time there are a number of onslaughts against its wellbeing, such as pollution, clear cutting, and over-logging. So we have to be deliberate in our actions or else we will, by definition, pass on to the next generation less than we received."

Raj ran his hand over Mark's desk as he asked, "Do you feel you own the earth?"

"Not in the grand scheme of things. We may own a postage stamp parcel here and there, but we don't own the earth."

"So does the government own it then?" Raj pressed on.

"Raj, I don't know how it works in India, but while the US Forest Service owns large swaths of land in the US, I am not talking primarily about ownership. It's about being a trustee or caretaker."

"Would you call it stewardship?" Teresa asked.

"That sounds like a good word for it," Skylar agreed. "Why don't you compare and contrast ownership versus stewardship of the environment—it would be educational for Raj and me."

Mark thought for a moment. "First, the concept of rights is different. If I view myself as the owner of natural resources, then I can do whatever I want with them. If I am a steward then I have to maintain or improve the asset. So if I had the right to use a section of wetlands or arable land, for example, I could not build condominiums there because sooner or later I need to hand it back in a pristine condition, and the condos would eliminate that possibility."

"Another difference," Teresa observed, "is the time horizon. Stewardship tends to have a much longer time horizon."

"How long might that be?" Raj asked. Raj had decided to play the uninformed Indian card to draw information out of them. He and Skylar were also keen to see how well Mark and Teresa played off each other.

Teresa picked up the conversation. "With ownership we tend to think in years, sometimes decades, but with stewardship things seems to be described in terms of generations."

"What about property rights?" Raj asked.

"That brings up another key difference, Raj. Owners are focused on rights; stewards are focused on responsibilities." Mark stood and paced as he spoke. "We train our customer base to think long term. We also do this when we explain our cost structure to them so that they think of the lifetime environmental impact of a bike, not the ticket price."

Mark and Teresa shared their care for the environment for the next fifteen minutes. Raj had been taking notes; he stood at the glass grease board to summarize. "Let me see if I got this straight..." and he listed the differences in two columns. They agreed with his synopsis.

"Now I have two questions for you as a couple. The first is this: which of these principles of environmental stewardship versus ownership apply to the company? Teresa, could you indicate for us first?" He handed her the marker.

Teresa looked at the list in front of her. It appeared to her that she and Mark had focused a fair amount on stewardship of the environment but had given scant attention to the concept of stewarding a company. Yet the parallels were clear. She marked them off.

"So do we agree quite a few of the principles apply to a corporation?" Skylar asked. Mark and Teresa agreed.

"My second question," Raj said, "is which of these postures is more suited to a company selling green bicycles: ownership, or stewardship? We don't want an answer now, but it would be good for you to debate this and get back to us in a few days."

Mark immediately sensed danger and wondered if this whole conversation was a set up. "Okay, we'll chat and get back to you," Mark said in a noncommittal way.

Skylar and Raj left the office. Mark waited until they were out of earshot then said to Teresa, "That was a set up!"

"Why? What was wrong with the conversation?" Teresa was a little stunned by the ferocity of his comments.

"Don't you see? If we say ownership is the right perspective, they will tell us there is a misalignment between our core business and our ownership philosophy. These guys are big into alignment. If we say that stewardship is the right model—multi-generational and all that stuff—then they will ask, 'So why are you selling the business?'"

She looked at him like he was being too suspicious.

"Teresa, I am whacked. Can we leave early and go home? Besides, Ken has given me some serious homework and I probably need your help."

Teresa waited until they were in the car before she looked at Mark and asked him, "What happened in the meeting with Ken?"

"T, he was a pretty straight shooter. He was not a smooth or schwarmy religious guy—just the same in person as he was in the pulpit, but a little more direct."

"What did he say?"

Mark relayed the conversation with Ken, and then got to the punch line. "Mark," he said "you are a Christian in that you got a ticket to heaven from Jesus; but you are a humanist who does business without God"... or something like that. "You are a Christian Humanist."

"And then?"

"And then he gave me a homework assignment, and told me to meet him back there, same time next week, if I have done the homework."

"That sounds pretty rude to me."

"Actually, it didn't feel rude, and I was not offended at all. It just felt like the guy read my mail... he nailed Kris and Whizz directly, then put words into the air confirming how I have been feeling."

"Did he say anything else that struck you?"

"Yes – he took a good look at our principles, asked me a few questions I could not answer, and then politely told me that they were common sense, but were not God's thinking. He tasked me with finding a Bible verse to support the key principles in each area."
"I told you they were Yogi Berra!"

"Well, he seems to be nicer than you. Besides, you are on the hook with me. Oh, and he emailed me when I got back to the office and told me to get my answers out of the Bible, not Google. I had already started looking on Google. It was weird."

Mark and Teresa had a cup of tea when they got home and figured they had an hour to dig into the principles before the kids came home. As they settled onto the sofa Mark asked Teresa, "Did I tell you I prayed in the coffee shop?"

"You prayed with Ken Jameson? In the coffee shop?"

"No, after he left I sat there and it struck me that I had offended God by saying I was in his club when, in reality, I kept him out of the business. So I apologized."

Teresa was surprised. "Well, well. Things are changing around here," she thought to herself.

They spent time looking for scriptures that could perhaps support their thoughts about the business, adding to Mark's earlier notes. They also got sidetracked into discussing new ideas on the different topics that were sparked by the verses they were reading. There was a verse about profit that said, "What does it profit a man if he gains the whole world but loses his own soul?"—that was pretty intense. They couldn't find much on product, but they did find produce, and also found some principles in concepts like "the work of God's hands," which sounded to Teresa like a product.

Teresa had to go out to a school function with Kelly, and Justin called to ask if he could eat dinner at a friend's house; Teresa had agreed. "Be home by 9 o'clock... love you."

Mark had the house to himself. Nice. He was still bothered by the whole stewardship conversation. They seemed to be questioning whether he had the moral authority to sell the company if the whole point of the business was a multi-generational impact on the environment. Mark decided to look to see whether the word "steward" was in the Bible. While he was at it he would check "owner" as well. He found that there were different versions or translations of the Bible online, and sometimes a null search in one version came up different in another. He found 24 references to steward or stewardship in the old school version, the New King James, and noted in the newer translations the word was now replaced with manager. So a manager and steward seemed to be similar. He concluded that he was not off the hook when it came to stewardship as the construct was clearly in the Bible.

He did the same exploration on the word "owner" and found a similar number of verses. There was a difference, it seemed, because when Jesus referred to an owner he was usually talking about God, not man. Mark wondered it if could be that God is more the owner and man is more the steward. He was no expert, so he would have to find out. He kept sifting through the verses by topic and tweaking his business principles, where necessary.

As Mark was reading the verses it was not just academic. There was something bothering him, and it suddenly became clear. "If I wasn't so bored at church and decided to engage with God on a Sunday, I would still have six days of the week to myself. But if God gets into my business then the whole week is pretty much shot. Even if I skipped Sundays, I would come out with the short end of the stick; God would get five or six days, and I would get one, unless I was guilted into going to church on Sunday as well, which was also more likely... in which case I lose the whole enchilada."

Then his mind moved to the conversation with Ken who told Mark that he didn't think much like God at all. Many associates in business who might claim to have a Judeo-Christian or ethical outlook flew past Mark's rearview mirror. Their worklife seemed unscathed by God. What about them? "What would I do if I were God?" Mark decided if he were God he would definitely grab businesspeople at work and be willing to forego a Sunday here or there.

"If I was God and decided to snag people at work, who would be my prime targets? The easy targets would be the individual contributors working in cubes. But the prime targets would be CEOs or business owners, for all sorts of reasons." As he thought this Mark got the sense he was in God's cross-hairs.

Mark found himself taking the internal discussion a step further. "What would be the surest way to get the companies to align with and promote God's agenda?" The answer was pretty clear to Mark. When a venture capitalist had a controlling interest in a company, whether or not they owned the majority of the shares, they often put a known commodity in as the CEO. Why wouldn't God do the same? If there were a way to get the CEOs who claimed to be Christians to demote themselves and make Jesus the CEO, he would have the controlling influence. Then he could teach them everything he knows about running the business.

Mark remembered Jameson had said God was in business. He went to the online Bible again and typed in business. Two things Jesus said struck him. The first was about being God's friend if you know his business. "I no longer call you servants, because a servant doesn't understand the Master's business. But I call you friends because everything the Master has shown me (about his business) I have revealed to you." It struck Mark as he read that statement: this book is an account about a man showing his direct reports how the boss, his Father, does business. There was another one-liner that was to the point. "Do business until I come back." He would have to ask Jameson what that meant.

When he thought about the reality of A-type, driven CEOs in cities around the world he wondered, "But why on earth would a CEO give up control of a company, relegating him or herself to the President slot, or lower?" It struck Mark how the issue was similar to the matter Green Cycles had been grappling with for many years. "Buy green, serve a bigger agenda, sacrifice now for a future return...trade money for a nobler purpose."

When Mark got to the Profit section he again came across this phrase: "Lose your life and you'll find it. What does if profit a man if he gains the whole world and loses his own soul?" Into his mind came the question, "What does it profit a man if he keeps his whole company, but loses his personal destiny?"

Mark had never relinquished control of his life to the God of Sunday. Now he felt he was being challenged to relinquish the control of his business to the God of Monday through Saturday. It was a much bigger challenge, and he knew the ramifications across the company and its stakeholders could be huge.

Out of nowhere the question came into Mark's head: "Mark, if you were God, would you leave Mark Green in charge of Green Cycles?"

Mark quickly washed it from his mind. "But I am not you. In fact, I don't think I even know you. I thought I knew the Sunday god, but I definitely don't know the God of Monday through Saturday."

22

Done!

Mark decided there was too much going on to wait to see Jameson next week. He took what he had from Teresa and the online searches and began making the notes more cohesive. He put two or three relevant verses in most of the 10 sections, although he still came up short in some areas. He added a couple of general sections on random words like business and company. He had not settled the conflict about who was going to be CEO of Green Cycles, and felt he should delay getting back to Skylar and Raj on the ownership-stewardship question until he knew the CEO answer. This seemed to be the pressing matter to discuss with Jameson.

When Teresa came home she was keen to talk. They engaged in some chit chat with Justin and Kelley in the kitchen before the kids went to their rooms. Teresa put some cheese and crackers together and came over to speak with Mark.

"You look cute... in a motherly sort of way," Mark teased.

Teresa ignored the compliment. "I have been thinking about the ownership-stewardship thing. It seems way more logical to me for us to be stewards rather than owners. As you said, how can we ask our customers to be stewards of the earth if we are not stewards of the company?"

"You could be right. But I have bigger problems." Mark didn't mean to minimize what she was saying, but had preoccupations of his own. "It seems, from looking into these verses, God is into business and Jesus' agenda was to show people how to do business the Father's way. If that is the case, then I would see no logical reason as to why God would leave me as the CEO of a company. I know precious little about 'Monday God.'"

Teresa looked at Mark. He seemed like he had encountered, stealing a line from the environmentalists, another inconvenient truth. Mark unpacked his Monday through Saturday line of reasoning with her; his main focus, however, was on the matter of who's the boss. "I feel like I have come home, found the title papers for the house in my desk drawer, and noted for the first time another man has his name on the title."

"What do you plan to do?" Teresa looked concerned. She was actually relieved, at one level, that Mark was finally tackling the question of his spirituality. It just wasn't happening the way she expected.

"I am going to call Jameson, tell him we are done with the homework, then lay out the other issues and see what he says."

"Don't you think we can just work it through on our own?"

"Ordinarily, yes. But we have the Due Diligence team more than halfway through their investigation, and I want to get this settled before we make a final decision. I have to."

Teresa agreed he should meet with Jameson again. "Before you do, I want to go over these principles again and make sure that I agree."

"With me?"

"No, on my own. I should do some of my own research."

Mark wondered if that was code for "I should talk to my girlfriends and mom about it" so he said, "Remember, these are our principles."

"Mark, if the principles are true, then they will stand up to scrutiny." She crinkled her nose as she said it, which was her non-verbal cue for "and there's no need for you to respond." So he didn't. Instead he started drafting an email in his mind to Jameson.

> *Ken,*
> *I have finished the assignment. It has raised some new questions. Can we perhaps meet sooner?*
> *Mark*

He decided this wouldn't work, so started again:

> *Ken,*
> *Teresa and I are all but finished the assignment. It will be done in the morning. It has raised some new questions, however. Can Edna schedule us sooner?*
> *Mark*

He preferred the second version because it mentioned Teresa, and left the "us" vague; us could be Jameson and him, or it could include Teresa if it happened that way. But he really wanted to see Jameson on his own.

"How does this sound?" He read Teresa the email.

"Yes, sounds good..." Teresa was absorbed in her review of his notes and was making changes.

The next morning Mark drove to the office on his own. Teresa had some errands to run in the neighborhood and told him she would come in later. Tamara looked flustered and followed Mark into his office. "That lady called again. She corrected my English, and told me Mr. Jameson will be here at 10 a.m."

"Nice..." Mark said, speaking Tamara's language for a moment.

"Do you mean nice that Mr. Jameson is coming, or nice that she corrected my English?"

Mark just smiled at her. He was actually thinking more the latter, but decided to leave Tamara guessing. He liked her, but had tried in vain to get her to speak receptioneze. "Tamara, let's look at my schedule...he pulled up his calendar. Can you please rearrange my 10 o'clock meeting? Push it out to next week if you can. Thanks."

Mark called Teresa and asked her to email him her latest draft. When he disclosed that Jameson was coming over she did not seem in a rush to join him. "That's nice—have a good meeting. Be sure to tell him I did my share of the homework," she teased. Clearly she was not feeling the same pressure he was.

Ken Jameson had instructed Edna to make time for Mark Green whenever he called because he had the sense Mark would be reaching out to him sooner rather than later. When Green's email arrived Ken forwarded it to Edna with a note. "Get me over there as soon as possible. Thanks." Edna liked a problem to solve—sometimes she liked a bit of drama, he thought, and would probably create more drama if she wasn't so married to her professional poise. If horn rimmed glasses were not fashionable again, Edna would probably have them. He decided to get a look at Mark Green in his natural habitat. People can tell you what you want to hear in a coffee shop, but when he met with businesspeople in their offices he quickly picked up how they viewed the business.

Walking into the receptionist area at Green Cycles confirmed this was the right thing to do. There behind the desk was Edna's opposite number: Asian, tattoos, pig tails, a plethora of earrings, black and white striped tank top under a sweater-like item that evidently doubled as a dress. Protruding from the bottom of the dress were stretch pants that ended at the calves, also adorned with tattoos, that found their way down to high platform cork sandals. The toe nails were a variety of colors, but black seemed to be the dominant theme. "Edna should see this," Ken thought to himself. As he walked up to her he was surprised to see her stand, stick out her hand and confidently say:

"Good morning, Mr. Jameson. We have been expecting you. How kind of you to come. Mr. Green will be with you shortly."

It was a stretch for Tamara, but she had been thinking about how to greet Ken Jameson in a manner that would send a good report back to the dragon who worked for him. This was the best she could muster in a short amount of time.

"Mark," Ken heard her say, "Mr. Jameson is here. Shall I bring him to your office? Okay."

"He will be with us shortly," she said, turning to him.

Mark could not risk the Tamara-chatter that might have ensued if she had escourted him, so he headed to reception as quickly as possible. After the usual greetings, Ken peppered Mark with questions about the business as they walked to his office. When they entered he noticed writing on the opaque glass white board: Ownership – Stewardship.

"What's this all about?" Ken asked Mark.

"Our Due Diligence team wanted a lesson in stewardship of the environment, so we outlined it for them."

"What was the point?"

"At the end of the day they asked two questions, which you see right there." Mark was pointing to the right hand side of the glass. Ken read the questions while Mark went on. "Personally, I can't help but think it was a bit of a set up."

"Tell me why, Mark."

"Well, as I explained to Teresa, my wife, if we say these environmental principles of stewardship, which is what we are touting, do not apply to the business, then they will say we are misaligned. If I say they do apply, shouldn't they be asking, 'So why are you trying to sell an asset that is a multi-generational trust?'"

Ken folded his arms and examined the list. It looked like a pretty good analysis to him. "So what did you tell them?"

"Nothing yet. In my mind I am, to be frank, delaying a response."

Ken didn't like it when people said "to be frank" because it made him wonder whether they were truthful the rest of the time. In Mark's case, he decided he was actually just being honest. "Why is that, Mark?"

"Well, I have to level with you and say that our conversation yesterday was a little unsettling on several counts. Since then I have been doing some thinking and I have to clarify some things."

"What part of our conversation bothered you?"

"When you said I was a Christian humanist..."

"Did I offend you?" Ken wasn't about to apologize, but he was curious to know which part of the phrase bothered Mark Green.

"Not really, but I think I may have misled you into thinking I was more Christian than I am."

Ken was trying to gauge whether Mark was just offering an apology, or looking for help.

"Go on..."

Mark went on to explain some of his thoughts from the previous night. "In doing my homework for you and reflecting on the events of the last week, I realized that I don't know the Monday God, and I barely know the Sunday God. I also don't think God would have me running, or stewarding, a company he owned."

"Before we tackle that question, Mark, I have to get straight to the point. Have you ever had a personal introduction to Jesus Christ?"

"What do you mean?"

"How well did you know me a week ago, Mark?"

"Not at all."

"How about today?"

"Well, I feel I know you somewhat, and I obviously think I can trust you with some pretty important information..."

"Thanks to Vera," Ken said. "She is a dynamo. Let's face it: you might not have met with me if a major shareholder in your business had not been in your face and required you to jump over this hurdle. Am I right?"

Mark thought about it for a moment. The conversation with Vera seemed like a long time ago, but it is why he agreed to meet with Ken Jameson. "You are right, Ken..."

"Mark, you trust me because you feel you know something about me, and perhaps because you first heard me speak in a church, so you also drew some assurance from that context. But the reality is we would never have got to this point without an introduction. Hence my question."

Ken saw Mark was listening so he went on. "Mark, you learned something about me from my talk, and you seemed to have learned something about God from your upbringing. But you didn't actually know me until we were introduced. Have you been introduced to Jesus and met him on his terms?"

"What might those terms be?" Mark asked.

"Before I tell you the conditions, Mark, I want to make one more point I have shared with many businesspeople. For too long we have told people that one day when they die and transition to eternity God will look them in the eye and ask, 'What did you do with my son?'"

"And is that true?" Mark asked.

"Reading the stories Jesus told about businesspeople I am convinced it is only one of the questions God will ask. The gist of what Jesus told people again and again was this: 'I am going away, I will give you assets to steward (as you say on your wall) and will be coming back again to see if you gave me a good return on investment.' It would be dishonest of me to introduce you to the 'personal Jesus' without sharing the other part of the picture. He is the 'all of life' Jesus, and will, if you get introduced to him, stake a claim to your whole life, starting with you, but including your business."

Ken was sitting across from Mark at the natural wood desk. He leaned in to make the point and watched Mark's response. He saw Mark drop a shoulder and tilt towards him, as if he was about to learn a trade secret. Ken knew something special was taking place, and shared candidly: "I think the devil is happy with people who spend Sundays in church, provided they don't take God into the rest of the week. Sadly, many church leaders are happy to have the businesspeople there on a Sunday, provided they leave their check at the door on the way out. Now, I am pro-Church in its fullest sense, and I love it most when it happens in an office on a Monday and in a living room on a Tuesday and at the gym on a Wednesday... you get my drift."

Mark slumped back in his chair as if he partly understood, and had just been validated in his thinking. It was a dim lightbulb moment. Ken watched him and let the truth sink in. Then he asked again, "Mark, have you actually met the 7x24 God?"

Mark straightened up, shot a glance to his office door, and asked, "Do you think you could introduce me?"

"Do you accept the whole package?" Ken asked as he looked in Mark's eyes, "Business and all?"

"Business and all," Mark said.

"Look at me, Mark..." when he made sure Mark was looking at him, Ken went on, "this here is my friend, my senior partner, and my Savior and Lord, Jesus Christ." Ken was motioning towards an imaginary person next to him. "Before you even got into business Jesus knew that you,

Mark, would get into so much debt there would be no way out. So he prepaid it. It cost him his life. Look at the nail marks here in his hands. Every time you missed the mark you piled on more debt. Every time you ignored him, did your own thing, or presumed all of this was yours, not his..." Ken motioned to the business around them as he spoke, "you piled on debt. But he is here, ready and willing to wipe it out on several conditions. First, admit you were running things from the wrong operating manual and commit to use God's, not yours, going forward. Can you admit that, Mark?"

Mark thought about his feeble attempt to describe his worldview and his foundational business principles and realized he knew little about how God would do things. He needed a radical revamp of his thinking, so he said, "I admit it. I screwed up."

"Good. The second condition is this: will you trust in Jesus here for both your eternal security, and for the day-to-day running of the business? Others trust in their intellect—many people here in Silicon Valley make a god of their minds—and some trust in some vague force-for-good. But will you trust my friend Jesus, who is the only one who died so that you don't have to, got you a permanent 'Get out of Jail Fee' card, and now is standing by to infuse you with his power so you can live life? Will you trust him only?"

"I will give it my best shot!"

"Mark, when you got married, did you say to Teresa, 'Hey, I will give it my best shot?' or did you make a commitment?"

"I made a commitment." Mark stood corrected.

"This Lord of the Universe deserves the same type of commitment."

"Got it. Thanks for the clarification. I am prepared to make a commitment to trust him."

"Excellent. There is one more thing before we make the handshake. Do you commit to discover his way of doing things, and to do whatever he

A Journey to Purpose

tells you to do? If you don't make this commitment then you may come back to me one day and say, 'Ken, I tried that God stuff but it was too demanding and it didn't work out.' Whatever God has taught me, Mark, I am happy to pass on to you if you agree in principle you will be a learner and a do-er."

Mark looked across the desk at Ken and the invisible man next to him. He didn't feel like he was getting a casual introduction to a business acquaintance; it was more like being called out to go to battle behind a serious leader. This was not the "Gentle Jesus, meek and mild, look upon this little child" stuff that he heard growing up. Ken was looking at him intently, waiting for his response.

"I commit to being a learner and a do-er." Mark said, with some trepidation.

"Whatever he says?"

Mark nodded.

"Wherever he tells you to go?"

Mark nodded again. Ken paused as if he was weighing Mark's response. After he seemed convinced that Mark was genuine, Ken stood up, and turned as if he were talking to someone at his side. Mark just stared.

"Jesus. I have a new friend, Mark Green. He is willing to enlist, and I would like to introduce you." Ken turned back to Mark and spoke.

"Mark. Up on your feet. Say after me. 'I, Mark Green...'"

Mark was on his feet and looking, not at Ken, but at the space next to him. He repeated after Ken, "I, Mark Green... acknowledge you, Jesus Christ, as the forgiver of my past, the surety for my future, and my new boss and friend. I hand over the ownership of my life, my wife, my family and my business to you. I make this solemn pledge in the Name of Jesus."

Ken looked at Mark, reached across the desk and grasped Mark's hand while he said, "Mark, your sins are forgiven, your wrongs are forgotten, and you are now a clean and free man. Jesus, to whom you have just been introduced, is not here physically, so he sent his Spirit instead. Receive the Holy Spirit." As he said the words Ken pulled Mark slightly towards him and, placing his left hand on Mark's chest said, "Thank you, Jesus, that you didn't leave us alone but sent the Holy Spirit to live inside us. Holy Spirit, fill your new son, Mark, right now, so that he can know you and live an empowered life. Amen. So be it."

Mark was not a very emotional guy, but he felt a little overwhelmed, a bit choked up. He managed to muster a "Thanks, Ken, I appreciate the introduction."

"My pleasure, Mark. This transaction is the most important business you will ever do in your life."

"It was a business transaction? Doesn't that demean something, well, spiritual?"

"Mark, business is spiritual. And you just swapped your debt for his equity. It wasn't cheap because it cost God everything. But you accepted his offer on his terms, and he has the matter recorded for eternity; the deal is sealed."

"How is the deal sealed?" Mark really did not know.

"Scripture tells us that the Holy Spirit is the seal. You now have the Spirit of God within you, and that, my friend, is God's seal on the deal." Ken made the supernatural sound logical.

"Alright, I think I understand," Mark said as he involuntarily moved his hand to his chest, "...but I do have a few more questions, if you have a moment."

"This is important; I have the time," Ken responded.

"Well, I have a CEO question. In our dialogue a moment ago we talked about giving the ownership of the company to Jesus, but I noticed that you did not mention who will be CEO."

"Mark, as I understand it, you don't own all the shares of the company. So you cannot make the decision unilaterally. You and Teresa should both be involved in the decision."

Ken's attention was drawn to someone coming towards Mark's office. Mark followed his glance to see Teresa walking down the hallway. She was wearing black slacks, sensible but stylish heels, a white cotton blouse and a bold necklace. Mark was momentarily distracted: "Looking quite corporate," he thought.

Teresa looked a little surprised because she had forgotten about Jameson coming to the office. What really caught her off guard was Mark's face. He seemed to wear a look of relief, or maybe it was something else, on his face. She shot him the quick "what's going on?" glance and walked over to greet Ken. "Ken Jameson, I am Teresa Green. I heard you speak on Sunday."

"A pleasure to meet you, Teresa."

"I liked your thoughts on God and business—I had not thought about it before."

"But what about God needing your business—how did that strike you?"

"I am not sure; up until now I have presumed God could probably get the job done without our business, actually. Business seemed to be more of a side show to a personal relationship with God."

"Interesting, Teresa. Mark was just sharing an interesting counter-point to that with me a short while ago. Why don't you lay your thinking out again, Mark? You will do a better job than me."

Mark was flattered that Ken would ask for his opinion. He sensed, however, he was being given some breathing room before explaining his new reality to Teresa. "T, I was explaining to Ken my musings about how much of the week God should get: if God took control of one's business then he would have a far greater slice of life than if he just got Sundays. We talked about this last night a little."

"Why don't you fill Teresa in on the rest of our conversation this morning?" Ken created the opening for Mark to share his introduction to Jesus.

Mark was having a little difficulty knowing where to begin. Teresa knew him well, and seemed to be happy with him the way he was. How was she going to respond? "Teresa, a week ago I did not know Ken. In fact, I hadn't even heard about him. After Sunday morning I knew something about him. Now we have met, thanks to your mom's introduction, and now I know Ken. At least I know him somewhat."

Teresa's head was turned at a slight angle, like she was observing him with a moniker of suspicion. He plowed on, partly because Ken had given him no choice, but more because he had began to sense a peace settling on him like a blanket. "Teresa, a lot has happened since I, thinking I was in control, put the company on the market. But my biggest mindshift has been the realization that I have had no real relationship with God, and my understanding of him his been inconsequential. This morning when Ken spoke to me I understood, perhaps for the first time, that I knew about God, but I had never met him. This left me with a vacuum in terms of how I viewed the business, life generally, and specifically our future. I was not hugely unhappy, but all the pieces did not fit together. Does this make sense?"

"Kind of...but what are you really saying?"

Ken watched the conversation and the couple seemed to have forgotten about him for the moment. Instead Teresa was searching Mark's face for non-verbal cues of what was happening with her husband.

"I am saying, Teresa, Ken asked me if I would like to be introduced to his senior partner, Jesus. I said I would, and he laid out the conditions. I accepted them, and Ken introduced me to Jesus. I made a commitment to serve him, and I gave him my life to be used under his direction. It was the only logical thing to do."

"So you became a full-on Christian?" Teresa asked.

Mark half-shrugged and held up his hands. "I am not sure about the label because historically I have associated 'Christian' with church and Sunday. I made a Monday to Sunday commitment to follow God and do what he wants."

Teresa turned to look at Ken. "And you think it is legit? You know businessmen—you don't think that this is because Mark is suddenly under pressure from all sides?" Teresa loved her husband dearly, but she also knew he was a problem solver and was good at finding a way through a difficulty. He had the Due Diligence people breathing down his neck, the pressure from her mom, then the diverging views of Kris and Whizz... she wanted some assurance this was not just an easy way out.

Ken didn't seem phased by her directness. "That's a fair question, Teresa, and one you should be asking. Anyone can make promises to God when squeezed. But I have a few reasons for believing that Mark has just had a genuine introduction to Jesus Christ. First, he did not take the easy way out."

"What would that have been?" Teresa asked.

"The easy way out for most men is to say, 'Honey, I will happily give you Sundays for the God-thing, but let me get on with the business without you.' It sounds crass, but few men understand that God expects their wives to be their partners. Mark understood that years ago, it seems."

"True. He has not excluded me from the business," Teresa agreed.

Ken detected she was not sold quite yet, so he continued. "The second reason why I think your husband is not looking for the cheap taxi out of the fire pit is this: he realizes if God is not Lord of his business, he is not Lord over the majority of his time. So by starting here, in this place of work, he has started where he has, apart from you and your kids, the most to lose."

Ken saw Teresa looking more softly at Mark. "If you need a third reason, Teresa..."

She was beginning to shake her head and tears were forming in her eyes, "if you need a third reason then I would point to the fact that Mark has grasped the essence of what he calls 'The CEO Question,' which is the matter of who is going to be in charge of the company. If he was bent on making a headstrong decision, then he would have delayed the decision until he had sold the company, assuming he could talk dear Vera into it, and pocketed the cash. Yet Mark just asked me when the CEO matter should be settled. I told him that it was a shareholder decision. And that is where you and your parents come into the picture."

Teresa sat down, taking it all in. Ken decided to wrap up his observations before he left. "Teresa, Mark, I am going to pray for you and then leave in a moment. I have prayed with many men in business before today, and I have to say your response to Jesus was as genuine as I have ever seen. So Father," he said still looking at them with his eyes open, "give this couple a fresh start in their marriage. Pour out your wisdom and grace on them as parents. Open their eyes to the incredible excitement of you at work in this business. Take up your residence in this corporation since Mark invited you here. Bless them so that they can be a blessing. And give them, of course, a new purpose."

When Ken gathered his things to leave, Mark and Teresa rose to say goodbye. They were both misty eyed. He reached for their hands and, taking them in his own, he spoke a commissioning over them, knowing they would not fully comprehend it. "Mark and Teresa Green, you are the appointed stewards of the Green Cycles household. You are called by God, and you are commissioned by him to be ministers right here. This is your parish, and these are the people entrusted to you. May God release to you every enablement of grace needed to live out your responsibilities. May you draw daily on the Spirit's power, and may you embrace friendship with God and partnering in his cause. So be it." He gave their hands a squeeze. They didn't fully grasp what was happening, but still tears were flowing down their cheeks.

"I will be in touch." With that, Ken Jameson left.

A Journey to Purpose

CHAPTER 23

Repurposing Business

Teresa and Mark sat in silence for about five minutes. It was Teresa who cut into the quiet: "What did he mean by the CEO question?"

Mark sighed, clearly feeling the weight of the moment. "Well, when Ken introduced me to Jesus, it was as if Jesus was standing in the room. I could not see him, but Ken spoke to him as if he was there. I realized I had held back from him what was rightfully his. If I was giving him my life, it seemed logical to give him the business. I asked Ken about who should be the CEO, and he told me it was not my decision."

"That's when he said you and I need to decide the CEO question together with my parents?" she asked.

"Evidently. I think his point might have been even broader; he did not want a flippant decision without thought for the implications."

"Do you think he is doubting whether we should sell the business?"

"I don't know, Teresa. But I realized last night, if I were God, I would not have Mark Green running this company. Even though I have some sense for the business, I have little clue about how it serves the bigger purposes of God. I barely know how it serves the bigger purposes of a greener, cleaner environment!"

"Mark, you know I have been a praying person, but my prayers have been mainly focused towards the kids and our home. I have not been unhappy with you; I have not been angsting or even praying much for you to change." Teresa was reassuring him that he was a good man.

"I appreciate your confidence, Teresa, and I do not feel in the least pressured by you. But I have sensed a growing hollow forming in my core. I felt like a tree where the outside looked good, but the older it got, the greater the emptiness at the center. Perhaps the vacuum has been filled today." They sat for a while longer, holding hands in silence.

"T, when Ken prayed for us, it struck me that we *have* to find out if God has a future purpose for this business. This is a crucial question."

That afternoon the Greens had a meeting scheduled with Raj and Skylar to gain feedback on their activities. They exchanged pleasantries, and Raj and Skylar appeared none the wiser about Mark and Teresa's profound morning. Mark decided to transition the conversation to a topic that had been on his mind since their lunch the previous week. "Last week you gave us some examples of companies that started well but had, perhaps, lost their course. I have two questions about this. First, what do you do about a company that has lost its purpose?"

Mark was surprised that neither Skylar nor Raj seemed to want to spend too much time on the topic, but still Raj responded politely. It was as if they had concluded Mark did not have too much clue about purpose, and they had moved on in their analysis to other topics. His response confirmed Mark's read on things.

"Not to beat a dead horse..." Raj looked down and arranged a few papers before continuing, pausing just long enough to let Mark know that he thought they were beating a dead horse. "I tend to think of three alternatives. First, if a company loses its purpose you can leave the company and hope it comes to its senses. Second, you can let it morph and follow the logical financial route, which could mean limping along, getting acquired, or shutting down."

"Why would it limp or need to be shut down if it loses its purpose?"

"That wouldn't necessarily happen. But what often happens is its better purpose gets replaced by a lesser purpose, namely, 'maximizing shareholder value.' Companies without a clear purpose tend to innovate less, and hence decline."

"What's the third option?"

"You can repurpose it."

"What is that?" Teresa asked.

Raj nodded his head to acknowledge the question and explained, "Repurposing Business is the process of helping a corporation discover its highest intended purpose, and taking deliberate steps to align every facet of the business behind that purpose."

"Is it the old purpose re-polished, or is it a new purpose?" Teresa looked for clarity.

"It is typically a combination of original and improved, like the household products you purchase: 'New and improved!' Somehow they blend the good of the old with the best of the new."

"May I add to my earlier question?" Mark asked.

"Go ahead."

"Which companies are candidates for repurposing, in your view?"

"Any corporation fulfilling a purpose that is less than noble is a candidate. The same is true for every corporation with a clear and noble purpose, but where the full resources of the company are not in line with that purpose."

"So, in my experience, that would include most corporations."

"Unfortunately, that is the case, Mark."

My second question is similar: 'What can be done with companies that had no altruistic stones in their foundations?"

"This is a slightly bigger challenge," Skylar entered the conversation, "but we have found one can often find traces of purpose if one does a bit of digging."

"What sort of digging do you usually do?"

"One place I tend to look is the passions of the founders. A common question that we ask is, 'What is your passion?' Occasionally we will have someone tell us they have no passions, but this tends to be the exception. Given enough time, most people will meander through likes and dislikes until they land on a passion or two."

"If they are not articulate about their passions," Raj added, "I tend to poke around for what makes them angry. I ask them directly, 'What makes you mad?' 'What makes your blood pressure rise?'"

"Take Green Cycles as an example: What do you think makes Whizz angry?" Skylar asked.

"Abuse of the environment." Teresa answered right away.

"That's right. You don't have to talk to him for long to realize maltreatment of the outdoors and disregard for the environmental community are his hot buttons," Skylar affirmed.

"How about Kris? What gets him going?"

"Disregard for process," Mark said.

"Breaking the rules," Teresa added.

"Any rules, or his rules?" Raj asked.

Teresa thought for a moment: "His rules."

"Did you sit down with them and have these discussions?" Mark was curious to know, mainly because they had not spoken with him on the topic.

"Actually, we didn't need to because their passions were fairly evident in our other meetings. Simply walking around their work area and chatting over meals made it fairly clear. If it was important, we could have explored it further."

Mark was hoping they wouldn't ask him about his passions. He needed some time to think it over, so he went to the next point.

"If passion and anger are not revealing, then where do you look?" Mark probed, looking for personal clues.

Skylar looked at Mark and Teresa and responded, "For me, I want to know if they had any dreams as children. I explore any ideals, any imaginings, any hopes that they may have forgotten about." She was looking for any flicker, any longings drawing a wisp across their eyes. She thought she saw something with Teresa.

"Purpose is also often multi-generational," Raj elaborated. "The problem in the Western mind is we embrace individualism, ignoring the baton in the hand of the previous generation. If you are royalty you don't wake up one morning and ask, 'Gee, what's my purpose?' Your purpose is to keep alive what your ancestors started. I like to probe family patterns."

"That is not very Silicon Valley-ish, Raj."

"If you look at the last 50 years, you are right, Mark. But this is a young State. Many countries measure in generations, not quarters."

"If none of this gives you any insight, then we go back to the question of personal calling, and forge a connection between a personal call and the corporate call. As you will remember, we touched on this the other day."

A Journey to Purpose

"One final thing," Skylar looked from Mark to Teresa, "truth is truth. It doesn't matter whether a company is founded for an altruistic purpose or not, or whether the founders had an awareness of what one may call 'universal truth.' The very fact that they are in business often sets them up to be aligned with a greater truth because they are in the business of meeting needs and blessing people... and sometimes whole cities and nations. The business they are in is usually an expression of a bigger truth."

"Can you give me a practical example?" Mark asked, "What about a company selling security software for computers? What does that have to do with God, for instance?"

"I will try. Why do people hack into computers?" Skylar asked.

"To destroy data, disrupt lives, or even steal intellectual property, I suppose."

"And what is the feeling you get when your ideas or identity have been compromised in this way, Mark?"

"Anger, outrage..."

"I think it is fear," Teresa said.

"So a software security company is countering fear, preserving property, and enabling people to do business freely, would you say?" They agreed, so Skylar went on. "I heard Jesus of Nazareth said his enemy came to 'steal, kill and destroy' and he came to give life to the full, and to remove fear. So can you see how the security company is aligned with God's business, whether they realize it or not? Their core purpose is consistent with God's core purpose, and the trick is to get them to discover it."

"Wow. So a lot of companies have the potential to be in God's business," Mark mused.

"The potential is there," Raj said, "but there is no guarantee they will discover it."

Skylar opened a folder of papers in front of her, effectively bringing the purpose conversation to a close. She pulled the Impact Assessment diagram from her file, and circled the areas that she and Raj had covered, quickly rattling off the departments and names of key people they had visited. "You are familiar with the aggregate gap analysis, shown on the summary spider chart here, but we may not have shown you the data sliced in other ways. Here you see it by department..." She traced her pen over the different lines, like a doctor reading an X-Ray, commenting on what the gaps might mean. "Your longevity charts are a little concerning, as it shows that your assimilation process has some possible weaknesses."

Teresa asked, "How do you know that by looking at this chart?"

"Do you see this green line... it represents the people who have been here for less than two years? Now on this page you see the same chart, broken down by department. Can you see the unevenness in the contentment level? This tells me your orientation and assimilation is done at a departmental level and people are not getting a full induction into 'The Green Cycles Way.' Newer people don't have the big picture."

"How would this impact the valuation of the company?" Mark asked.

"It pushes it down. Whoever buys you will look at these gaps and figure out how much it costs to fix them. When departments and people within departments are not singing from the same song sheet, it costs money. Our observations are not about how good people feel, but what it costs to get them to be a high performance team. And you, better than most businesses, should understand high performance teams. Which cyclists are important on a team in the Tour de France, for example?

Get our point?"

Raj and Skylar walked through a few more areas, reported back on progress, made some allusion to a softer valuation, and scheduled a follow up session. Mark was finding it hard to focus on page after page of charts. He was thinking about the purpose of Green Cycles in light of his morning encounter. While they were speaking Mark had made notes by doodling a mind map. He wanted to unpack it. He was also trying to remember if he had dug up any verses on purpose that might give him some pointers.

"So it's agreed then. We will meet in a few days to talk about whether we want to proceed," Skylar was saying while Mark was dreaming. "Mark?"

"In a couple of days then – just have Tamara pencil it in. Thank you."

Mark smiled as if he was pleased to see them leave, but really he was eager to chat with Teresa about purpose.

"Honey, can you remember all the things they said about purpose? They didn't seem too interested in it, but I made some notes here..."

Mark turned to a fresh page on the flip chart and created a diagram summarizing their process on how to dig up a company's purpose. "Teresa, are you up to doing this now? Can we take a first pass?" Mark looked like a game show contestant who had been given a fresh crack at the big prize.

"I need a cup of tea first," Teresa replied. "I will get something for us and be back in a few."

By the time she returned to his office Mark had plastered the wall with flip chart pages. She saw her name on the top of one page, his on another, and "ours" on a third. "These three pages are the trails to explore if we don't have a purpose. The other three pages on this side are the haystack—if we once had a purpose but lost it along the way, then we look here."

They each took a different color pen and started jotting down key words next to each branch of the map. The conversation went back and forth, but after a while Teresa said, "Mark, this is good, but it could be pointless. All of this may be for naught unless we somehow get God's perspective on purpose. What does he even say about purpose?"

"Where?"

"In the Bible, remember? Did you find anything on purpose?"

"I seem to remember it came up quite a few times... let's take a look." Mark pulled out the pages from the night before and looked for the verses he had found on purpose. He seemed to remember they were generic, and none of them talked about starting a cycle manufacturing facility. Nonetheless, he had copied them into a document and noted his questions or observations next to each one. Now he read the quote and his notes to Teresa.

> "The Lord made everything for its own purpose..."

"So, T, it seems everything has a specific purpose."

"Mark, do you think this applies to a company too?"

"It's a good question, but it does say 'everything' so I think bicycles and businesses are fair game. Here's another one," Mark, said.

> "I know that you can do all things, and that no purpose of yours can be thwarted."

Mark contemplated silently, "If God will be unthwarted, what difference does it make what I do or don't do? Will he not automatically do whatever he likes with the business?"

"That's encouraging, Mark. If we are honest in looking for what God wants, it seems he will not be stopped in his purpose."

"But doesn't this verse make it sound like we could just be pawns in his game? I am not sure what the line is between him doing whatever he wants, and our role, Teresa."

"That's a good point... I don't know either. Let's go to the next truth."

> "Many are the plans in a man's mind, but it is the Lord's purpose that prevails."

"So," Mark pondered, "could it be that God's purpose trumps my plans?"

Teresa interrupted his thoughts. "So your question is whether God's purpose supersedes our plans? I think that is what it is saying. But it doesn't seem to tell us what his purpose is, right?"

"That's one way of looking at it, Teresa. But what if it is saying, 'Mark, no matter how dumb your plans are, if you want my purpose, it will happen.'?"

Teresa looked at him and said, "I guess that would be a plus."

> "And if...you will not obey me...your strength will be spent to no purpose"

"Hold on: does this mean that my life on earth will be a waste of energy if I am not obeying God? That's what it seems to be saying." Mark began to explain his question. "T, when I looked at this line I remembered the cloud I had been feeling not so long ago. I think it could have been the 'Cloud of No Purpose.'" He made quotation marks with his fingers as he said it. His face looked like he was revealing something personal, so she prompted him with a nod which told him to go on. "Well, I clearly still don't know my purpose, let alone the purpose of the company. But since Ken prayed for me the cloud has gone. Gone, Teresa." He was a little choked up as he said it and added, as he looked back at the paper. "I somehow don't feel my strength will be 'spent to no purpose.'" He tilted his head back and forth as if to say, "And that's a fact." She just observed. "Okay, T, next one."

They spent some more time looking at each of the purpose verses Mark had found. Some verses were clear, and some more obscure, but she had the sense that they were collecting puzzle pieces that would later come together.

"I cry out to God Most High, to God, who fulfills {his purpose} for me."

"The net is God says he has a purpose for the man who cries out to him," Teresa concluded.

"But the Pharisees and experts in the law rejected God's purpose for themselves..."

"What? The religious guys rejected God's purpose for them?"

"For if their purpose or activity is of human origin, it will fail."

"This is a scary one; if my purpose or activity is from me, it will fail. Is that a hard and fast thing, I wonder?"

"For when David had served God's purpose in his own generation, he fell asleep; he was buried with his fathers and his body decayed."

"Wow!" Mark said, "Here is a guy who got to the end of his life and it was clear that his purpose was fulfilled. How can that become true for me?"

"With this in mind, we constantly pray for you, that our God may count you worthy of his calling, and that by his power he may fulfill every good purpose of yours and every act prompted by your faith."

"Wait a second: there seems to be a leap in this verse. How do we get from me fulfilling God's purpose to God fulfilling my purpose?" Teresa asked.

They went back and read more of the story of the people who were getting this letter from a man named Paul, and the people seemed to be going through a lot of suffering for God. It seems they were genuine people. Perhaps this suffering is what aligned their purpose with God's purpose.

"In a large house there are articles not only of gold and silver, but also of wood and clay; some are for noble purposes and some for ignoble. If a man cleanses himself from the latter, he will be an instrument for noble purposes, made holy, useful to the Master and prepared to do any good work."

"So whether you eat or drink or whatever you do, do it all for the glory of God."

"This sounds like a catch-all phrase, but I honestly don't know how to do it... I mean, I don't know how to design a bicycle or run a business 'for the glory of God.'" Mark said.

"Still, Mark, this seems to be a key verse." Teresa was pensive.

"Agreed. Perhaps we should go back over the pointers Raj gave for discovering Purpose and see what we come up with."

Mark and Teresa had a good conversation, but this was new territory for them. They were not used to digging through scripture to find business solutions. After about an hour Mark said, "I feel better, but my concept of what God wants to do with the business is no clearer."

Teresa smiled a cheeky smile and said, "That's progress."

"How can that be?"

"Mark, two weeks ago you didn't even think God had a purpose for the business."

CHAPTER

24

Loose Ends

Teresa was beginning to wonder why Skylar had asked her to come into the business. She had enjoyed some of the sessions, and it seemed good for Mark to have her around while they were processing the option to sell the company. Teresa was also thinking about Mark's turn for the better, and she wanted more time to get her arms around it before continuing down the sale trail. They had little choice, however, since the Skylar/Raj mandate was nearing an end and they scheduled more meetings where they expected her to attend.

"Oh, there you are," Tamara said to Teresa. Tamara seemed unaffected by the fact that Teresa was the CEO's wife. "The Skylar lady was looking for you. You have a meeting over with the finance guys."

"Thanks Tam," Teresa said.

Tamara squirmed in her funky outfit a little. "Gee... only my mom calls me Tam. Thanks." And off she went.

"Where did Mark find her?" Teresa wondered to herself, "She lives in her own world."

Teresa learned a few things in the finance meeting. Margins were going to get tighter, it seemed, and the outlook was uncertain. The steady growth they had enjoyed over the years was not guaranteed. The conversation instilled in her a new urgency to make a decision about selling and she wondered whether Mark's instincts had, in fact, been correct. She finished the meeting and headed into his office where he was working on email.

"Mark, we have quite a few loose ends to tie up. Can we not just take a look at the things we are working on and try to bring some of them to a close?"

"Sure, when do you want to do this?" Mark asked.

"I actually just need some time on my own to journal before I look at any more maps or tables or charts."

"That's fine. I need to get some exercise anyway."

"I will head home; we can have dinner at about 6 p.m. I will think about the loose ends and we can chat this evening." She got up to leave. "See you later." She walked over, kissed him on the forehead, and was gone.

Mark hadn't exercised in days, so he walked through to the indoor cycle track, pulled on some exercise gear, and spent 20 minutes doing some laps. Much of the rest of the day was consumed in meetings, but at the back of his mind was the experience of being introduced to Jesus and looking at what the Bible had to say about purpose. The issue was not that he was resistant to what it was saying, but that it was a new topic to him and he did not fully understand it. He wondered how many other topics there were he had little clue about.

Teresa took a walk through the neighborhood when she got home and enjoyed the gardens and the summer flowers. This whole experience with Mark seemed surreal. A few weeks ago her life seemed normal and safe, but now Mark had thrown everything into a tailspin. It seemed, if she was honest, more neat and tidy to have God for Sundays, and let Mark just go to work, get the job done, and provide for the family. Now there were all of these questions about purpose and what religion had to do with the business. As she made her way back towards the house she wondered whether this was a phase, or whether this was the start of a whole new direction for her.

Although Teresa was a pretty practical person, she was not the obnoxious type who used pragmatism as a blunt object to cajole others. Back at home with a cup of tea she pulled out a note pad and began to list the areas where she felt there was too little clarity. "God," she breathed, "I need some clarity." Immediately after, she said it a phrase came into her mind. "No you don't. You need trust and obedience." She was a little shocked—was that her imagination? She didn't dismiss the thought, however, and wondered what it meant. "Can't I have some answers too?" she half-asked, half prayed. Another phrase came to her mind, and she was pretty sure it was from the Bible.

"If any man lacks wisdom, he should ask God..."

Assured that it was fine to think, but cautioned that this was more than just a mental exercise, she made a list of areas where she felt some further insights were needed.

When Mark came home she felt somewhat refreshed by the time she had spent alone. "How was the rest of your day?" she asked him.

"Anything exciting?"

"Not much—how about you?"

"I had a quick walk around the neighborhood, checked in on rides for the kids, and made a list of loose ends. I think we should at least put them on the table before the kids come home; that way we can get our minds around them."

"Sure. Let's do it." Along the way Mark had learned that when Teresa and Kristoff had a list there was no sense pretending to be in charge of the agenda. Was it strange he thought of them in the same sentence?

A Journey to Purpose

TERESA'S LOOSE ENDS
- Ownership, stewardship
- The CEO question
- Household
- To sell or not to sell?
    - Timing
    - Do we know enough?

"Teresa, you have a pretty long list here. Maybe you can pray for us before we get going."

Teresa was not used to a husband who wanted to pray, but suppressed her surprise. She was sure they would not be doing all of this had the whole due diligence process not forced them to work together. She was torn between the benefits she was seeing and the private thoughts she had on her walk about the normal life and the white picket fence.

After she had prayed Teresa looked at Mark. "I was pretty troubled by the conversation about stewardship the other day. I feel we have spent more time worrying about stewarding the environment than stewarding the business."

"Are you saying I have not been a good CEO?" Mark asked.

"Not at all. What I am saying is our cause has been the environment and we have been vocal about it. We think and talk like stewards of the environment because it is so much bigger than us. Clearly we don't own it, and we just do our bit to make it better and pass it on to the next generation. But when it comes to the company we have thought, or at least talked, like owners."

"Well, at this point we do own the company, Teresa."

"Mark, we own our house, but the city has rules, and the state has taxes. We cannot do with it as we please. We are restricted in how big and how high and how ugly we can build. We own it, but the city planning commission has a pretty big say."

She went on. "Technically we own the company, but I think the analogy of the environment applies. Perhaps we have been missing the big picture that all business actually belongs to God, and we are just managing this one for him."

"Interesting... the part of the stewardship discussion that bothered me was the contradiction between what I espoused as our stance of caretaking the environment, versus my view of owning the business. The two models are out of sync. I think I agree with you."

"Mark, what are the benefits of us not owning the company?"

"We would have fewer problems," he said. "I mean, technically we would still have to deal with things, but it often seems easier to deal with someone else's problems... so maybe I would get less stressed. What do you think?"

"I think it would give us fewer choices. If we really decided the company is God's, then he gets to call the shots. We would have less scope for going out on a limb with far reaching decisions."

"Would that take the decision to sell the business off the table?" Mark asked.

"I don't know. I do know, however, that we would have to think a lot more about the long term and not just about the immediate future. We enjoy great rides through Redwood trees because conservationists like John Muir thought generations ahead. Yet when it comes to business we seem to think in years, or maybe quarters and months."

"That's true. There's another thing that is bothering me, Teresa. When I made the contract with God, you know, with Ken Jameson, I gave God my life."

"Go on."

"What I actually said to Jesus was that I hand over the ownership of everything to him: you, the kids, the business, the whole lot. It was obvious that, since he had paid for it, it was his. I have thought about it a bit more, and that doesn't mean we cannot sell the company, because if we do, we will have a healthy sum of money which we can also steward for God. But it does change my stance in the decision making."

"So how do you think God looks at us now?"

"Teresa, I think he sees us as stewards, not owners. That's pretty clear."

"And you think, Mark, we have the option of stewarding money or..."

"People. People are a big part of it. We are talking about the future of managers, employees, families... and our kids. One way or another people are affected. Our cause, if we have one, is a part of it, but I think it is bigger than the environment."

"So are you saying the choice we have is having influence over money, or influence over people?" Teresa asked.

"That's the way I see it. Of course we could start or buy another business, but if we just hand the money over to a money manager then we greatly curtail our opportunity for influence."

Teresa looked at Mark. He seemed to be shifting, developing a new perspective. "That's not all," Mark continued, "if what Ken said about God needing our donkey is correct, then we have to take into account what selling the company does to our broader stakeholders."

"Such as..."

"Our customer base: there are thousands of them. Then there are the environmental groups: most of them will never be in a church on a Sunday because the outdoors is their church. If our business could be a way to impact those who interact with us—those served by our products—then we have to seriously think about what happens if we gave up that influence."

"Have we made a decision, then? Have we determined we are stewards, not owners?" Teresa asked him.

"I cannot see it any other way. Those stories Jesus told, the para-things.."

"You mean the parables?" she clarified.

"Yes, the parables. I read a few the other day and he pretty much told the guys, 'Here's something for you to look after, I am going away for a while, and when I come back I expect to see it in better shape than when I left. If you don't make it grow, you are in trouble.' I think the same applies to Green Cycles."

"What do we do now? Can we formalize this in some way?"

"I think we can settle it among ourselves, but it takes us into your next question, and for that we need to speak to your parents."

The Greens pulled up to Joe and Vera's house half an hour later. "Mom, dad... good to see you." Teresa gave them a hug. Vera was eyeing Mark a little suspiciously. She barely greeted him, not to be rude, but just because her mind was buzzing. Mark must have talked Teresa into a sale. Once they had settled into the small living room with its many stuck-in-the-60's furnishings, Mark shifted in his chair, squared up, and looked across at Teresa's parents.

"Joe, Vera, I would like your approval to demote myself." Mark began his quickly prepared speech.

"Not so fast—what are you talking about?" Vera shot the statement off as less of a question and more of a return volley she had pre-packaged, no matter what he said.

Mark and Teresa looked at each other, and he decided to work Ken Jameson into the picture. "Vera, you asked me to meet that Ken fellow, and I did. In fact, I met with him twice this week, and the second time we met he introduced me to Jesus." There was no visible response from

Vera and Joe, so he continued a little awkwardly. "Keeping it simple, for the moment, Teresa and I are convinced that if God actually owns the company—the donkey, remember?—then he should be the CEO. So I would like to demote myself, with the permission of all shareholders, and just be the President."

It sounded a little weird even to Mark, and seemed to raise more questions than it put to rest. Joe raised his eyebrows, and Vera searched Mark's face like someone reading a map, looking for clues. "So if you were the President and God was the CEO, would you still want to sell?" Vera cut to the bottom line.

"Well, actually, I don't think it would be our decision as much, because we are realizing, after lots of thought, that we are actually more stewards of the business than owners."

"So, let me get this straight. You kids are saying that God is not only the CEO but the owner of Green Cycles."

"At least of 70% of Green Cycles... you can hold your 30% however you wish—that's your prerogative, Mom and Dad." Teresa tried to smooth over Mark's attempt at clarity.

Joe spoke for the first time. "Teresa, you and Mark are in this together?"

"100%, Dad..." Joe was giving her a look that asked another question. "And I don't think he is losing it, or anything. I believe this is a significant and genuine change." Teresa felt like she was re-introducing Mark as a potential suitor. There was a moment of silence as Joe quietly weighed what he heard.

Vera broke the silence. "Mark, you have pretty much satisfied my first requirement which was that you and Teresa be in sync. My second question had to do with your purpose." She wagged her somewhat bony finger back and forth between Mark and Teresa as she spoke, indicating she was talking about their purpose as a couple. "Have you figured that out yet?"

The truth was that Mark and Teresa had spent so much time on the business that they had not talked about their joint purpose.

"Mom, we are still trying to find out the exact purpose of the business, especially from God's perspective."

Mark chimed in. "Good question, Vera. We think that our purpose, together, is connected to God's agenda for the company. If everything is supposed to be for his aims, then it has to fit within his..." Mark was waving his arms, trying to grabs words out of the air, "...we are trying to figure it all out."

Vera decided to let their non-answer slide. They had made more progress than she had hoped. As a mom, she wanted to hug Mark and re-welcome him to the family. As a shareholder, she wanted to make sure they were thinking straight. Shareholder Vera won out.

"Fine," she said, "keep thinking about it. Meanwhile," she reached for a piece of paper as she spoke, "Joseph and I have signed the Director's Minute. It's all in your hands."

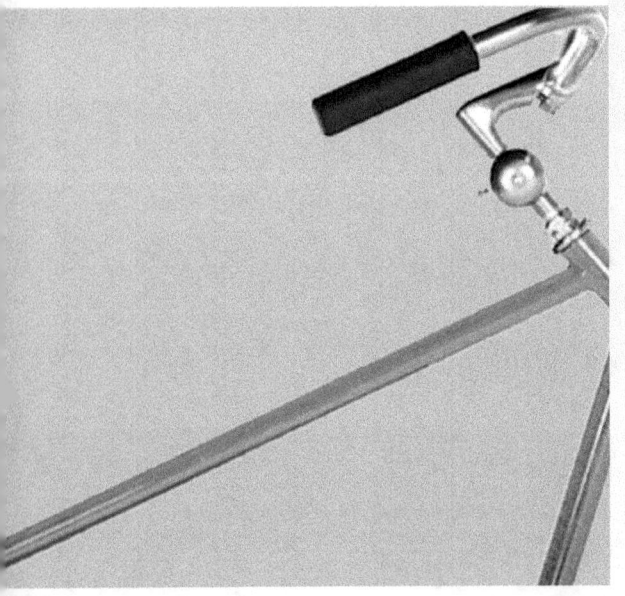

CHAPTER 25

A Great Offer

The Greens left Joe and Vera's home with an agreement in principle that it was unlikely they would sell the company, but they had the signed Director's Minute anyway. It had been on the list of loose ends from the night before, and Teresa wanted it out of the way. Vera had said, "I will continue to get prayer for you, but at the end of the day you have to do what is right for all shareholders. And that includes us, kids."

Driving home, Teresa prayed out loud. Mark glanced over at her as her face grew bright and dark as they drove past the street lights in Los Gatos. She was hardly aware of him; she was just talking to God. In the past it seemed they had been self-conscious when they prayed together. The pressure of the last few weeks was acting like a paint stripper on an old bicycle; awkwardness around spirituality and prayer was the victim.

"God, just give us a sign or something. We need to know we are heading in the right direction. I don't want this to be just Mark and me making things up..."

This was the first time Mark had seen Teresa doubting whether they were on the right track. Surely she should be happy he had entered into contract with God, as he thought of it. She should be relieved he wasn't about to sell the business they had built together and forfeit the possibility of the Green family achieving its full potential.

"Please give us a sign." She repeated.

They got home. "Split the kids?" Mark asked.

"Sure – I'll take Kelly," Teresa replied.

Teresa went to Kelly's room, sat on the end of her bed and asked some questions about her day. "How was school? Do you have any new music for your iPod? How are the girlfriends? Any unusual plans in the next week or so? A party? What kind of party?" When Teresa was satisfied that there were no unusual indicators, she kissed Kelly and said goodnight.

"Hey, dad. What's up? You look a little different." Justin was giving Mark a good perusal.

Mark smoothed his hands over his shirt looking down at himself. "Same old, same old," he said as he shrugged and looked at Justin.

"I mean your face. Anyway, how are Gramps and Grandma?"

"They are good... feisty as ever. They should last quite a while longer." Mark hoped he was not saying it with any regret in his voice. But the parting comment was still on his mind.

"How about you—did the guys like those LED lights?"

"Oh! Yeah... thanks. They like them a lot."

"When's the trip again?"

"Not for three weeks."

"And whose dad is taking you—Greg's, right?"

"That would be Javier, dad."

"Pretty close—they both start with a G."

"No they don't…"

"I'm going to bed, Justin. I am wiped. Give me a hug." He didn't wait for an answer but instead walked over and hugged his son. He had decided a while ago that he was not going to follow the norm of avoiding physical contact with his teenage kids; awkward or not, he would hug them. This evening was not awkward.

"Night."

Mark lay in bed feeling pretty good. In his mind he ran through a list of reasons why he felt good: the kids seemed to be doing fine, they had decided on a course of action for the business, Vera was all but satisfied, and, mostly, he finally felt like the other shoe had dropped spiritually. A dangling uncertainty, had been come to rest. When Ken placed his hand on his chest in the office… it was pretty weird, but it was real. And Mark knew something had been settled, once and for all. Now all they had to do was close the loop with Stephens & Sanchez, have them call off the dogs, and that would be it. He fell asleep before Teresa was done with all of her illogical nighttime taking off and putting back on preparations.

Mark was pretty chipper in the morning and decided to cycle to work. "I'll take the bike, T, and see you later in the office. We have that meeting with The Duo tomorrow and should spend some time preparing."

As Mark pedal-powered to work he thought about the best way to break the news to Skylar and Raj. Perhaps leaving it to S&S was a little discourteous and he owed them a better explanation. But he would need to check in with S&S just to make sure he was following protocol. He showered and went to his office, glanced at the mail on his desk—nothing unusual—then plowed into his email while eating a power bar. There was an email from Sanchez with the words "Directors Minute" in the subject line. He opened it and gave it a quick skim.

> *Mark.*
> *Just confirming that you have the signed Directors Minute. I need to meet for 15 minutes. Call when you get a moment.*
> *Carlos*

"At least it isn't Stephens," Mark thought to himself. A moment later he felt a twinge of guilt. "That wasn't very nice."

"Carlos... fine thanks. It is going well. Where? At the Starbucks on Pine—which one? There have to be three on that street. OK. Fifteen minutes."

Mark took one of Green's electric vehicles and drove to meet Sanchez, who was already there when he arrived. "Mark, how is the DD going? Any surprises?"

"No, it's going well thanks. Nice people, pretty thorough."

"Well, I have a pleasant surprise for you. We have another offer for the company."

"You have another offer—what kind of offer?"

"Well, I cannot tell you who the potential acquirer is, but I can say this: they are one of the major manufacturers wanting to open a green line, as they call it, and would rather buy your outfit than start from scratch. They have already come up with a valuation, since they know the industry, and they are ready to do a deal."

"How much will they pay?" Mark found himself asking.

"They have given me a range, subject to a little homework, but it is handsome."

Mark stared at Sanchez, trying to figure out if he should press him for a number. Instead he went the roundabout way, "Well, Carlos, that's nice but I have grown pretty fond of the present suitors. They seem to have the heart for the business."

Suddenly Sanchez was a little defensive. "But do they have $15 million of heart? And will they offer you a $1.5 million bonus to stay on for two years to guide the docking into the mother ship?"

"Maybe they will—did you and Stephens talk numbers with Skylar and Raj?"

Sanchez shifted a little awkwardly. "To tell the truth, they were a little unusual. Their MoU told us little about them, and we can't find out much more for another week."

"Why is that?" Mark was genuinely curious.

"They said their standard procedure was to not discuss terms or who hired them for the first three weeks. After that, if they are interested, they will reveal more," Carlos explained, shrugging his shoulders. "Mark, getting any offers in this economy is amazing. We had to take their terms. Besides, hold them off for one more week and their initial inquiry period is over. We have no obligation to renew. Then you take the new offer, and you are home free... plus the $15 to $20M in your pocket. This kind of offer doesn't come along often, Mark. What do I tell them?"

Carlos Sanchez looked across the table at Green. He hardly knew him, but he did know how to read a man's face. Initially there was the suspicion, which was normal, then there was the curiosity phase, followed quickly by the rapid realization that he would have more money in the bank than he ever dreamed possible. The excitement phase was generally followed by the cool negotiator phase, and Green followed the pattern. So he played along and threw out a few numbers, and quickly Mark was hooked.

"I will have to check with my wife," Sanchez heard him say, "we have done a lot of processing and I have to check with her. It could be fine, but I don't know for sure."

This was not in Sanchez's playbook. He thought to himself, "You're a grown man, a big boy... you are a CEO. We are not talking about selling your kids here." Instead he smiled at Mark and said, "Okay—get back to me, but don't say anything to the other guys...Skylark and the Indian fellow."

"Skylar and Raj," Mark corrected.

"Yeah, whatever. We have one week until they are gone. Think of them as bait on the Green Cycles hook. They have attracted the big guy and that makes the time with them worth your while. Don't call me until next week," Sanchez timed his exit to coincide with the last sentence. He placed his somewhat chubby hands on the table as he nudged the chair backwards with his butt. When he was standing he shook Mark's hand and left the coffee shop. "Not until next week," he said again as he left.

Mark sat stunned for a moment. He took his cell phone from his pocket and twiddled it in his hand, round and round and round. He opted to wait for a face to face with Teresa to share the good news. She had asked for a sign, and this seemed to be a $20 million sign. "Wow, this God stuff is amazing," he mumbled to himself as he left for the car.

To his surprise, Teresa was already in his office when he arrived. She looked happier than last night when they drove home, and wore clothes to match her mood. He kissed her cheek, air style, to avoid messing up the morning paint job, as he called it, and said, "You look cheery."

"Mark, I am. I cannot tell you how much peace I feel since the decisions we made yesterday. We are just stewards, Mark, not real owners, and these people are not just employees but extended family. I even had this motherly feeling towards to the place when I came in here today, something I have not felt for some years!"

"But you asked for a sign..." he said incredulously.

"I know I did, but I don't actually need one. In fact, this morning I read a verse that says something like, 'it is a wicked generation that asks for a sign.' Mark, I don't want to be wicked; I don't need a sign."

Mark should have been delighted, but all he could think about was the $15 to $20 million Sanchez had assured him of, and how convincing Teresa was going to be a hard job. He would have to introduce some reality quickly.

"Teresa," he started off carefully, "last night you prayed for a sign, right?"

"I have already explained that, Mark" she said, as if he didn't hear her the first time.

"Well, this morning when I came to work there was an email from Carlos Sanchez, of Stephens & Sanchez. He asked to meet with me urgently. I just met him, and another buyer is offering us a lot of money to buy the company."

Teresa paused, looking penetratingly at him. "That seems to be irrelevant, Mark, because yesterday we just decided to keep the company."

"Teresa, what if all of this other work was just preparing us to sell for a better price?"

She squinted at him as if she had just heard something stupid through a morning fog, but wasn't quite sure.

"What I mean is this: Sanchez explained the first company is what baited the hook for the second company, a major player in the industry that wants to start a green line, to come after us. It is a perfect set up."

"It could be a set up alright, but I am not happy about it. What did you tell him?"

"Actually," Mark paused for effect, "I told him I had to check with my wife." When he told Sanchez this he had seen a small look of disgust on his face, but now Mark was particularly glad he had said it because Teresa seemed to be in a fighting mood.

Teresa was aghast as she looked at her husband. He seemed to have gone from seeing clear principles the night before to seeing dollar signs this morning. He had even walked her parents through some of the guiding principles that they had been working on, explaining why the business should be in God's business, and not in someone else's hands. Then she had an idea.

A Journey to Purpose

"Mark, why don't you take out the principles we talked about yesterday, honey... the ones you shared with Mom and Dad... and talk me through how they apply to the offer from Suarez."

"Teresa, it is not even an offer yet. He said we should just stall Skylar and Raj, then the due diligence period will expire, and to contact him next week."

"About what? Mark, the only contact we should be having is to say we no longer want to sell the company! Did you tell him that? No, you didn't." She could see from his face that he had not told Sanchez about their decision, so she pressed in. "That could have been another item off our list, closing that door, and instead you came home with a bigger opportunity."

Mark said nothing because she had a point. But he still thought opportunities like this don't come around often; it was a lot of money. He had to get Teresa to taste the enormity of it before she just dismissed it out of hand.

"We could do a lot for our kids with that much money... and your parents would get a nice $5 million or so. Remember what she said... do what is right for all the shareholders."

Nevertheless, he reluctantly printed off the list of things they had agreed upon the day before. He was pretty sure that the Bible could be read more than one way, so he decided to go through the principles and see how they held up in the clear light of real money. He and Teresa had narrowed it down to two or three principles for each of The 10-Ps.

Area	Principle or verse

Purpose
- The business is here to get God's work done.
- The idea is to please God with why, how and for whom we run the company.
- "Whatever you do… do it for the glory of God."

Product
- The product should meet the big goal of minimizing a negative impact on the environment.
- We will explore other groups that God might want us to serve with our expertise. (Don't know what that looks like yet.)
- We will figure out how to collaborate with God more on the product side, discovering creative solutions to things God cares about

Positioning
- We will make sure we are not saying one thing and doing another.
- We will figure out how to be green and clean.

Presence
- We stick by our principle of no unsavory marketing.
- We will try to find out how to have God's presence in the business if there is a connection to marketing. (There is a verse about, "if your presence is not with us, then we don't want to go")
- "In your presence is fullness of joy" – if God is at work, our employees should be happy.

Partnering
- We will partner with God. (Ken says we are junior partners; what is this exactly?)
- We will find out who else God is partnering with and try to work with them.
- M&T will be partners, practically. He won't make big decisions without her, and she will not have less say than Whizz and Kris (clean this one up a bit, but it is important.)

Process
- We will ensure processes are honest, clear, and consistently applied to everyone inside and outside the company.
- We will not let process be a big stick, nor absence of process be a big swamp.

People
- We will embrace our responsibility to care for, guide and shape the thinking of the people in our sphere of influence, finding appropriate ways to bring them under God's influence.
- We will be a family, and treat people accordingly.
- We will strive to make work and home come together in a healthy way.

Place
- We will run the business in a sustainable way.
- We will make the business more welcoming of family members. (T's idea)
- We will try to make our values more apparent across the board. (eliminate cheesy posters, etc.)
- We want the place to be around for the next generation. We don't want just a story, but we want a legacy. (Too many places come and go in the Valley.)

Planning
- We will include God in our planning. (remember Asa, Old Testament king)
- We will pray before we decide, especially big things.

Profit
- We will have a bigger definition of "the bottom line" – profit, environment, family, community, etc.
- We will evaluate things in light of eternity, not this month or this year, or even this decade.
- We will try to give God a good ROI. (What is this, exactly?)
- We commit to not sacrifice our long term "thing" for short term convenience.

Mark had printed two copies and passed one to Teresa. As he glanced at them they did not look very elegant, but they were starting to capture some of what was important to them as a couple. He and Teresa were also somewhat guessing at what might be important to God; since he was unofficially the new CEO, his ideas should be on the list.

"Let's use this as a checklist, Mark, and indicate whether we would violate any of these things on the list if we sold, for whatever amount of money."

"How do you want to score it?"

"A check means the principle stands, even if we sell, an 'X' means we could not do what we said if we sold, and a '?' says we don't really know. Let's rate them separately then see how close we are."

Mark expected that the statements would be a little horoscope-ish, and he could get them to mean whatever he wanted, not that he wanted to manipulate things, but $20 million was a lot of money. He didn't just want to abide by some platitudes if they were not holding water. He began going through the list.. "Check, not-so-sure..." Mark got through his list fairly quickly and glanced across at Teresa.

Out of the corner of her eye Teresa watched Mark dart through the principles, pouncing from point to point like a cat whose live meal was about to escape. He killed it, but didn't eat it, plopping his pencil down on the desk as if to say, "Done!" She did not look up, only slightly raising one eyebrow after she knew he would be looking her way. A short while later he picked up his pencil again, apparently re-checking his test, playing with his mouse-food.

She, on the other hand, was in no rush. If Mark wanted her involved, then he would have to let her process things her way. It was awkward, but she ignored him gazing periodically in her direction, pretending to be mulling a deeper meaning he was not quite sure was there. His left leg jiggled, something he did involuntarily when antsy.

Mark easily saw that Teresa was in no mood to hurry into his $20 million decision. She was like a tourist on a jog through new scenery, pausing at the pinnacles of The 10-Ps to look at vistas she had read about in a travel magazine, but never really seen herself. Every now and then she had an "I see you now" look on her face, as if she had snatched a glimpse of something emerging from a mist... views that she knew from the catalogue should be there.

When Mark returned from getting them both a cup of tea he watched her set her pen down and reached for her Bible. "Howzit going?" he asked, casually.

She took the question seriously and paused to look at his face while she took the piping brew. She had recently found a verse on partnering that was pretty amazing to her as a wife. In an obscure book a prophet had recorded grievances God had with the nation of Israel. She never knew God complained about men not partnering with their wives.

Mark and Teresa talked through their evaluation of the list of principles. She had suggested they discuss all categories except Partnering, asking to end with her new-found discovery. Mark shared his Purpose rankings, and she responded. Then she shared on Products, and he chimed in. There was plenty she and Mark agreed on, although she thought he was making assumptions about how employees having broader opportunities and more financial stability would perceive an improvement in their lives. "They could have a temporary boost, Mark, but who is going to be looking at the eternal perspective for them? I have been spending time with different departments, getting to know the people again this past week, and I am not convinced they will be better off as part of some large corporation."

When they were finished going through the first nine categories she looked at him as lovingly as possible and said, "Honey, let's make this easy. How did you rate the third item under Partnering?" She leaned forward to see Mark's list as she asked. *M&T will be partners, practically. He won't make big decisions without her, and she will not have less say than Whizz and Kris...* He had a check mark next to it. "Mark, I take your rating to mean we cannot make a big decision to sell the company if the two of us are not in one mind about it." She didn't wait for an answer, but went on. "I uncovered a verse that confirms this, and it is really a warning to husbands and wives." She read it aloud, inviting Mark into her find.

> Another thing you do: You flood the LORD's altar with tears. You weep and wail because he no longer pays attention to your offerings or accepts them with pleasure from your hands. You ask, "Why?" It is because the LORD is acting as the witness between you and the wife of your youth, because you have broken faith with her, though she is your partner, the wife of your marriage covenant.

"Mark, we do not, in my view, need to have a huge debate about this decision. Yesterday we agreed, as one, that we should be stewarding the company as God's managers. Today you seem to be wavering, and I am not in agreement with you. So, as I understand it, we cannot proceed with a sale, regardless of the price."

Mark looked at Teresa in disbelief. What part of the $20 million was it that she did not understand? It could radically change their lives. They would have investment options. He could retire early, and her parents would be set financially. It was not a straightforward matter at all. He had already been daydreaming about getting a small cabin at Tahoe, and it was high time he upgraded to a hybrid. So, he might have to work for a few years for a boss he didn't like, but after that... She was definitely oversimplifying the matter. He needed another man's perspective.

"Can we call Ken Jameson and get his counsel?" Mark asked.

"Sure," she said slowly, "but bear in mind we cannot go to my parents and get their hopes up, and we cannot speak to any of the staff. Agreed?"

"I agree—Ken or no one."

Mark put a call in to Dame Edna who answered with her usual efficiency. "Oh, how long will he be gone? Ten days... Thanks, Edna."

A Journey to Purpose

Teresa watched Mark's face—it reminded her of the person who made the get-out-of-jail phone call to find no one home. He hung up, looked at her... "I guess it's just you and me."

"Mark, we can do this," she said with some assurance.

They did agree this was not something they could get into at the office. "Mark, I am not sure that we can go through this list of principles every time. I imagine that there has to be some better way to make decisions that we can learn, perhaps some common ways in which God guides people. I will do some research on this, and you can clean up the principles. Looking at it again it seems that we need to at least add in some key scriptures."

Mark looked over his calendar for the day. "I am afraid that I have a meeting that runs through 5:30 p.m. so I won't be much help today. Why don't I pick up some Chinese food on the way home so that we free up some of your time. I will be back with food by 6:00 p.m."

"Thanks... but before I go, can we pray together? Have you yourself paused to ask God about this? You just committed to make him your boss—I suspect this means letting him guide the small and large decisions. I don't want to leave here with tension between us."

Mark looked at Teresa who had a plaintiff expression on her face. She was not being difficult or obstructive, only eager to try to do things the right way.

"You are right—go ahead."

"Mark, I know you are not much of a prayer guy, but you will have to learn quickly because we have some huge decisions to make and we cannot do things based on common sense or gut instinct. You have no problem speaking with me, so it should not be much different speaking with God. Please, you take the lead..."

Teresa was looking at Mark who looked like a cyclist with an uncomfortable saddle. She took his hands and closed her eyes so he didn't feel she was checking him out. And she waited.

"Hchm…" Mark cleared his throat as if he was going to make an important announcement. "God, Mark here again, from Green Cycles…" as if God had to look him up in a database and sift his name from all the other Marks. "Yesterday I gave the business to you. Today someone else wants to buy it for a tidy sum. Teresa thinks the answer is no, and I think it is a lot of money. We need you to weigh in on the matter, and I am not sure how you plan to do it. Whatever you have in mind, please let us know pretty quickly. That's it for now. Amen."

"Thanks, Mark." Teresa seemed to be proud of him and came over to give him a hug. "See you at six. Call me if anything important crops up with The Duo. But let's try to avoid them until tomorrow."

Teresa had an appointment with a girlfriend, Melinda, whom she had known for many years. Melinda had a quiet confidence and a relationship with God that had been deepened by difficulty. Her husband, Jack, had been laid off after working as an engineer for a semiconductor corporation and had decided to try his hand as an entrepreneur. Unfortunately he was more dreamer than businessperson, had failed to settle on a specific product, and exhausted the family's finances. By the time he was back in a regular job they had a significant amount of debt. Melinda sought counsel, and decided to ask God for her own business ideas. She had started an online business selling craft products to a niche market. It didn't look fancy but it was profitable. In the process she had learned many lessons and tended to approach interactions from a considered perspective. She and Teresa caught up on the basic news while they ordered their drinks—a soy latte and dirty chai—and then found a quiet table. Teresa, cupped the dirty chai, and poured out her heart. As she drew to the end of her story she confided, "Melinda, it feels like a roller coaster. I thought we were agreed, and then this new offer came along and it has seriously affected Mark. It's as if he is viewing everything through $20 million lenses."

Melinda backtracked on the conversation. "Teresa, God seldom, if ever, gives us a challenge without having already tooled us up to meet it. I can already see how you and Mark have taken some steps that have positioned you to handle this. For example, he is speaking with you—you know what is going on in his head."

"Probably because my mom pressured him..." Teresa reacted.

"It doesn't matter why he is talking; take it at face value and stay in communication," Melinda counseled. "The second thing is this: the business minister, Kent, was it...?"

"Ken. Ken Jameson," Teresa corrected.

"Ken directed Mark towards scripture and Mark has taken that seriously. I don't know too many people who are searching scripture for God's perspective on business."

"That's true—Mark is like a boy with a new toy digging up verses in the online Bible."

"The third thing preparing you for this is the discussion about the purpose of business. If you can get that right, then it will be safeguard against all sorts of distractions."

"But Melinda, we are pretty clueless about what our purpose really is!" Teresa objected.

"The good news is you know you need a purpose that fits in with God's purpose. It's a good place to start. Do you want some advice?" Teresa nodded her head.

"Set aside the lists that you and Mark started a week ago, and first find out what scripture has to say. I had to ask God some pretty honest questions after Jack failed at business, and yet I felt the way out was for me to go into business. That took faith."

"How did you do it?"

"I pulled key verses speaking about money, business, work or wealth. (Bear in mind we were broke.) I then extracted the principle from the verse, and asked 'How can this apply to me?'" Teresa was looking at her intently, so she continued. "I saw in Proverbs 31 that a woman did all sorts of income producing things. The principle I pulled from there is that women can be breadwinners too. The application was easy: find something that people need, that I enjoy making, and sell it to them at a profit. Other verses were more obscure."

"Such as...?"

"Proverbs says, 'Let another man's lips praise you, and not your own.' The principle I drew from the scripture is that I should not toot my own horn. The application was vaguer, so I prayed, and realized customer referrals would be a great way to have other people praise me without me sounding off."

Teresa spent a few hours with Melinda who seemed happy to share what she had learned. They hopscotched scriptures and principles, leaving Teresa to work out the application at Green Cycles: business, obedience, faith, listening to God, and a whole lot about wisdom.

"Thanks, Melinda. This has been invaluable." Teresa had no idea that her time with Melinda would yield so much.

"The bottom line, if there is a bottom line, Teresa, is that you and Mark have begun the process of searching and submitting to the higher authority of the Word of God. That, my friend, is a safety net for you both."

When Mark returned from work they enjoyed a family mealtime, focusing on the kids and what was happening in their lives. After Justin and Kelly headed off to do homework Teresa recounted her afternoon coffee with Melinda. Mark was surprised Melinda knew so much about God and business, but he was tempted to discount it because she ran a small operation. When Teresa shared the specific scriptures and the related principles Mark had to admit that her rationale was solid.

"Of course, we have to think through the application at Green Cycles," Teresa explained, "but I learned a lot."

"It looks good. Did she say anything about decision-making?"

"She encouraged me that you and I are at least communicating and are together on this."

"What did she think of the your partnering verse you put on the table this morning? Does she think you have veto rights in decision-making?"

"She didn't put it that way, nor did I, for that matter, but she pointed me to a related verse that says that God will bless us when we are in unity. She also stated pretty frankly that men would lose less money if they listened to their wives."

"She should know," he said less than charitably, "but in my case, I am trying to make us a whole lot more money." Mark quickly got back to the $20 million offer.

Then Teresa dropped to the bottom line. "Mark, the more I read these things and think about the principles, the more peace I have about keeping the company, and the less comfortable I feel about the new offer."

"Let's look it up!" Mark said.

"I don't think you will find 20 million in the Bible, Mark." They had been speaking for a long time and Mark had pulled up verse after verse using online tools to either augment, or question what Melinda had said.

"I am sure there is stuff about peace..." he was half listening to her, not realizing it was a joke.

"There it is: 247 verses on peace! Let's start at the back this time. A lot of them seem to be a greeting... they sound like they are from Santa Cruz. 'Peace, brother, peace.' Here's a different one. 'Let the peace of Christ rule in your hearts...' Let's check it out in a few more translations because I don't always get the first one. Ouch! Listen to this one. "Let the peace of Christ keep you in tune with each other, in step with each other.'"

They seemed to be onto something with the peace topic. "Let's try the next one: whoa, this guy, Amplified, has a lot to say. Get a load of this!

> 'And let the peace (soul harmony which comes) from Christ rule (act as umpire continually) in your hearts [deciding and settling with finality all questions that arise in your minds, in that peaceful state] to which as [members of Christ's] one body you were also called [to live].'"

"Read that again, please Mark."

Mark read it again, slower this time.

"So, Mark, it sounds like it is saying, at the end of the day, one can make a decision based on the absence or presence of peace. I wonder if that is right? Why would that be?"

"T, there are over 200 verses on peace here. The answer probably lies out here," he motioned to his computer screen as he continued, "in this whole pile of peace verses." Mark scanned the list. Some were about war and peace, others about peaceful. Then a familiar verse caught his eye. "Hey, here's the Christmas one.

> 'For to us a child is born,
> to us a son is given,
> and the government will be on his shoulders.
> And he will be called
> Wonderful Counselor, Mighty God,
> Everlasting Father, Prince of Peace.
> Of the increase of his government and peace
> there will be no end.'"

Teresa saw it. "Peace is the name of Jesus, and peace comes with his government, got it? Governments make rules, as far as I know. So when he is making the rules, we get the peace."

Mark did get it. "So that's why that Colossian guy said 'let peace act as umpire' because it indicates whether we are letting Jesus call the plays." "So you are saying that my gut instincts are right?" Teresa asked.

A Journey to Purpose

"No, I am saying that your gut instinct is more likely to be the peace of God playing umpire... 'Safe!'" Mark was motioning like a baseball umpire, "You are out of here!' Something like that," he smiled. Then he looked more serious. "Teresa, I would really like $20 million—or even less than $10 million after paying taxes and your parents. But I definitely want harmony with you and probably peace with God even more."

"Probably?"

"I am just being honest: I don't know him as well as I know you."

"Mark, it is Friday evening and I am wiped out. How about we take the weekend off and pick this up again on Monday? I have had enough processing..."

The rest of the weekend was spent doing routine chores, interacting with the children, and avoiding the heavy conversations of the week. Mark seemed to be reflective, perhaps settling into his newfound identity. Teresa wondered about pushing for them to go to church on Sunday, but she did not need to, as Mark himself suggested they attend the early morning service. The crowd was older; she noticed Mark still looked awkward in that setting. Would that change? Should it? While they were not doing any heavy thinking, she was still preoccupied with the events of the week. Was she right in asking Mark to walk away from financial security?

On Sunday evening Mark broke into the do-not-talk zone and suggested they have a family meeting with the children over breakfast. Teresa agreed.

CHAPTER

26

Withdraw

Justin and Kelly dragged themselves out of bed early. It was rare that Dad and Mom called for a family meeting, but never before could they remember one on a school morning. By the time Justin got to the kitchen there was a pile of hot pancakes ready for the taking. He dug in, momentarily forgetting the family meeting. His dad broke into his thoughts.

"Kids, your mom and I..." always the official announcements seem to start with "Your mother and I..." so Justin knew it might be important. On the other hand, it might be something as inconsequential as a change to the family talk plan on their cell phones.

"You may have noticed that we have been really busy with work these last few weeks..."

Justin didn't know whether to acknowledge their busyness, or pretend he didn't care. He was non-commital. "Yes... whatever." He said it with a smile, which would keep them guessing. "Yes, I noticed!" or "Yes, I don't care." It was good speaking a different language.

Dad droned on. "Confidentially, which means that you tell no one, not even your best friend, we were considering selling Green Cycles." Justin looked across to see how Kelly reacted. She had a sleepy, maybe bored look, but he wondered what she was really thinking. Often she pretended not to care, but was impacted by uncertainty or change more than he was. "We could have got a lot of money for it..." Dad meandered on, "but instead, we gave it away."

Justin and Kelly stopped chewing and snapped their heads around, as one, to gawk at Mark. The studied teenage disinterested haze was gone.

"To who?" Justin asked, incredulous.

"To whom..." Teresa corrected.

"Dad...Mom," Kelly looked at her dad first, then her mom.

"Kids, I resigned as CEO and we gave the company away." They stared at him; he looked at them and smiled.

Teresa looked across at Mark. They had not discussed how they would include the kids in the discussion, and clearly Mark was using shock tactics to get their attention. And he had it.

"Dad, why did you give it away... I thought I would work there one day," Justin said.

Mark explained the events of the last few weeks, including his encounter with Ken Jameson. "I realized, if I were God, I would stake my claim, not just to me and my life, but to the company too. We had lots of conversations about the difference between doing a business for ourselves, and doing it with God to fulfill his bigger purposes. So, we gave the company to Jesus, and we are planning to formally invite him to be the CEO. We are going to be stewards, not owners, and to manage the company for the good of future generations."

When Mark left the room to get some papers from his briefcase, Kelly looked at Teresa and asked, "Mom, is Dad losing it?"

"Yeah, Mom, is Dad losing it?" Justin repeated, still trying to take it in. Just then Mark came back into the room. "Think of it more like a trade, Justin, not a loss. When you have a battered, low value skateboard or bicycle, and someone comes along and offers you a trade for a brand new, lifetime warranty, top of the line version, for free—would you take it?"

"I think so," Justin said, looking for the catch.

"Well, that's what happened with me. I had a small, Sunday-only idea of God that had nothing to do with Monday through Saturday. I had no idea God was interested in our business. Then I discovered he wanted our business to be his business, and the best thing was, we decided, to give it to him."

"But how is God going to run the business, Dad?" Justin still was not convinced.

"I think he is going to keep us on as managers," Mark said.

"So everything will be the same then," Kelly chipped in, "except you will change your title."

"Actually, we have a lot to learn about doing business God's way, and we are only just beginning to discover that we don't have a very good idea what it looks like," Teresa clarified.

"You haven't been cheating on your taxes and stuff, have you?" Justin asked.

"No, Justin, the business has been run ethically, but the whole way of thinking about business has been from our perspective, not God's, and we have to learn a new way of seeing things."

"Kids, a key thing that will change is how Mom and I make decisions; we plan to involve God a lot more in our decision-making, and we hope to include you too."

Teresa loved the blend of colors in the Los Gatos gardens. The school morning traffic gave her ample time to take in the variety: dark California oaks backdropped low maintenance grasses and puffy annuals. Whisteria draped lazily over the grand porch of an old Victorian. The weather was even kind to the transplanted Aspens poked by unimaginative home remodelers in triplets in sand islands on front lawns.

"I think that went pretty well," Mark said as he navigated the back roads.

"Well? You nearly gave them a heart attack! What was the 'we gave the company away' tactic?"

He smiled. "It will teach them to pay attention at the dreaded family meetings."

They spent the rest of the drive talking about how they would break the news to Skylar and Raj that they would no longer be selling the business. Mark made a note to check the agreement with S & S to ensure there were no legal issues. He called Tamara and asked her to let The Duo know he and Teresa were running 15 minutes late. When the Greens walked into Mark's office Skylar and Raj were engaged in discussion about other businesses and didn't seem phased.

"Good morning Teresa, morning Mark. How are you today?" Skylar made the greeting long enough for her and Teresa to simultaneously check out each other's outfits, like polite poodles on a Saratoga sidewalk.

"Sorry to keep you waiting," Teresa offered, "we had an impromptu family meeting with our kids." She seemed satisfied with her relative choice of clothing.

"About the sale of the company?" Raj asked.

"Sort of," Mark interjected, "we brought them up to speed with where we are personally, and so on."

"Speaking of the personal side of life, Raj and I have noticed that the Due Diligence process has stirred up lots of discussion; we know this can be challenging. So we would like to get a sense of how you guys are doing. To accomplish this we have another assessment allowing you to do a self-evaluation on the front wheel of the bicycle. We mentioned it earlier, and now is the time to complete it." Skylar was friendly, but left no choice.

Raj handed them a document that was similar to the Impact Assessment, but the categories were different. "Let's take about half an hour and talk you through it. Once again, rank each statement twice to indicate Importance and Performance. Let's start at the top with Fitness."

Doing an assessment was not top of Mark's list, but Raj plowed forward and they were soon drawn into the content. After some discussion of each category they arrived at the last area: Faith. As he looked at the statements Mark felt his heart pounding in his chest, and he knew he would need to tell them about his new encounter with God. He did not really have good language, certainly not the proper religious sounding words, so he decided to just tell them in terms he knew best.

As they looked at the statements Raj asked, "Can either of you tell me why we would ask Faith questions in a business context?" Mark and Teresa looked at each other, weighing how to proceed. When they did not answer immediately, Raj pulled a coin from his pocket. "Faith and risk are two sides of the same coin," he explained. "One cannot be in business and not have risk. This means that business involves faith, and we need to have some understanding of your view of faith because it impacts not just your outlook on things, but whether you have hope for the company. On the other hand, people can use faith as an excuse for being sloppy, not doing their work, and leaving everything up to some 'higher power.' So, we want to get some perspective on where you are."

"It's funny you should mention it, Raj, because a month ago I would not have understood what you are saying, but today I have some inkling." Mark was obviously choosing his words carefully, and weighing Skylar and Raj's response.

Skylar slipped into the conversation. "Just so that I get the trajectory: would you say faith is more or less important to you than a month ago?" Mark could not tell whether she was supportive or not, but he tossed caution behind him and said, "More important."

A Journey to Purpose

"Mark, are you just feeling more optimistic, more faith-filled about the company... or is there something else going on?" Raj, for the first time, seemed a little intense.

"There is indeed..." Mark's palms were feeling a little clammy, but he had not finished the sentence when Raj shot back,.

"Is it going to impact our work negatively, because we have invested a lot of time and are coming towards a favorable conclusion."

Mark looked across at Teresa. He suspected she was praying, not out loud, but something was going on. He then looked at Raj and Skylar and said, "I had a visit from a new friend, and he introduced me to a special friend of his who has an interest in Green Cycles."

"There is another buyer?" Skylar asked in disbelief.

"Not him, no..."

"So there is someone else then? Mark, we have an exclusive for 21 days," Skylar continued.

This was not going the way he intended. Mark raised his hand with a "calm down" gesture and said. "Not so fast. Let me share my story. Skylar, Raj, you asked lots of questions about purpose, and this got me thinking. I met with a man who knows something about the real purpose of business. The friend he introduced me to is Jesus Christ."

Things went very quiet.

"He has not offered cash for the company, but when I said he could have rights to my life and career I realized pretty quickly that maybe I did not have the authority to sell the company without his consent."

Raj bobbed his head from side to side, Indian style, in a gesture Mark did not understand. "I hear you. No problem." For the first time Mark thought he heard the trace of an Indian accent. "So, did you ask him? Can you sell?"

Teresa leaned forward. "Raj, it's not that simple. It's not like walking down to the Finance Department and asking how much money is in the bank."

"In India there are many gods. So I understand about spiritual things. But why would God want you to keep your business... couldn't you do lots of good things with some money? Do you know how many orphanages you could build with the money you will make from the sale of Green Cycles?"

Mark and Teresa looked a little exasperated, wondering how they could explain things better.

Skylar came at things from another angle. "Mark, Teresa—there are lots of fine people who have sold their companies and gone on to do good charitable work."

Mark tried again. "I don't think I am making myself clear, partly because I am not very clear. Teresa and I have thought about it and realize we could do some good with a pile of cash, but we would no longer have influence on so many people. We have a huge customer base, environmentalists and many others who don't seem to have much contact with people of faith. If we sell then we would probably forfeit that platform."

"If you make a sizeable donation to the Sierra Club, Mark, you will have a huge open door," Raj shrugged as if it was pretty simple.

"Raj, what about our employees? These people are like a family, and we can make a difference in their lives. With respect, if you bought the company how do we know what would happen to them?"

"They are talented people, Mark, and are quite capable of finding employment elsewhere," Raj said. For the first time it struck Teresa they had not had any real conversations about what the buyer would do with the employees if the company was sold. Raj continued, "People are a resource: you use them to build the business. Besides, if we outsource a few jobs to India..."

"Actually, Raj, I don't think that's the right way to look at it. One of the principles we have thought about is interdependence: people will only build the company over the long haul if the company is building the people."

Raj countered with a profit perspective. "Teresa, you know how thin the margins are. The bottom line is the bottom line, right? You cannot waste too much money on people."

"Raj, Skylar—we don't have all the answers, but we are pretty convinced the bottom line is not the bottom line. You know we have at least a double bottom line of financial return and environmental impact. But we are figuring out we are not just building bikes to save trees; we are building people who will make products that have an impact for future generations."

"So you have gone from tree hugging to people hugging," Raj was half smiling. "But, seriously, if you lose your focus it could have a negative effect on your valuation."

"Raj, we don't think it is the best thing to sell," Mark looked him in the eye.

Skylar peered from her pile of papers like she had just heard a brand new piece of startling information. If she wore glasses she would have pushed them scrutinously to the end of her nose. She had been eyeing the Greens to see how settled they were in their new conclusion. She decided to press them from a different angle. Skylar glanced at the binder of papers in front of her then said, "Look, this is a good little business, but it is not exactly rocket science. A large competitor could enter the field and you would be at risk. Your profitability could take a serious hit. Isn't this the time to exit?"

"Skylar," Teresa paused to make sure she had her eye, "what would you think of someone who was in business just for the money? Everything I know says that people should work for what they are passionate about, not just for money. Why should it be any different for us now? Shouldn't we be pursuing our passions?"

"Okay," Skylar seemed undeterred by Teresa's passionate questions. "Let's assume you work because of passion. In our meetings, to be brutally honest, I have not seen a whole lot of passion for the business. What's changed?"

"What we are trying to tell you is we are discovering that Green Cycles is more than just a business. The company can be used by God to make a difference in the lives of many groups. If we sell, we lose a unique opportunity."

"What's so unique about your customers?" Raj asked. "They are people who buy bikes."

"That's not the way we see it any more. Our customers are people who have bought into a cause, and our bikes are part of their passion. We sell a purpose — preserving the environment — and they join us in that purpose by buying green. We have already won the price/purpose battle. What if we sold a bigger purpose?"

The tone of the meeting seemed to warm. "Go on..." Skylar said.

"We also sell the multi-generational, long term view. We know how to do this. What is a longer viewpoint than eternity? We could be uniquely positioned to get them to make the connection between long term environmental thinking and very long term spiritual perspectives. Both simply involve cause-related, implicational thinking."

"This could be interesting... but what about your employees? Do you plan to get them to some church?" Skylar asked.

"Well, our employees are family, but they are eclectic. I don't think there is much we or anyone else could do to get them to a typical Sunday church. They cycle on Sundays, and their only pew is in a coffee shop or on a log... maybe even a saddle. What we have thought about thus far is what we can do to make sure they encounter truth, in a natural way, in their work setting. They will not go to church, but we wonder whether God could come to work."

"Did you say God would come to work?" Skylar quizzed aghast.

"Well, if you bought the business wouldn't you come here?" Teresa asked. "In my mind, when Jesus paid the price to buy men and women back for his Father, that price was big enough to buy their careers and businesses too. And so, if God has bought this business, then surely he would want to be here. We may be naive, but it does seems logical to us."

Raj looked intently at them. "So, let me get this straight. Mark has been introduced to Jesus. This has met some personal spiritual needs he has, but has now spilled over to how you are both thinking about the business. Not only do you not want to sell, but you want to make this God's business? Anything I missed?"

Somehow things had become clearer to Mark as he and Teresa explained things to Skylar and Raj. Even their pushback made him more convinced than ever keeping the company was the right thing to do. And when Raj asked, 'Is there anything else?' Mark responded.

"Yes there is, Raj. I am resigning as CEO. I plan to stay on as President of Green Cycles, but we plan to formally invite God to be the CEO. I know it sounds weird, but to us it is an important decision." There was a long pause.

Skylar looked at Raj who returned her considered stare. Their silent debate hung in the air. Mark reached for Teresa's hand and gave it a "Well said... we are doing the right thing" squeeze. When she and Raj had apparently reached an agreement on what to say next Skylar turned and very deliberately said, "We hear what you have said, but please give us the courtesy of one more meeting. It should take 60 minutes. Whether we remain involved with you are not, we have observations and recommendations for you."

Mark felt the pendulum of the good breakfast meeting with his kids had swung and crashed into the glass wall of the due diligence duo. Did they think he was flip-flopping? Had he strung them along? He was marginally embarrassed by being seen as doing a "bait and switch." When Raj and Skylar left the room he and Teresa prayed. Soon his feelings were outweighed by something greater: the peace of clearer conviction.

A Journey to Purpose

CHAPTER 27

Wheel Alignment

When Mark and Teresa met with Skylar and Raj the next day he noticed they were wearing the same outfits they wore on day one. It had been less than three weeks, but it seemed much longer. Raj sported the French cuffs and gemstone cufflinks. Mark meant to ask Skylar about the feather pin. He looked at them and thought he would miss the odd couple. But he would not miss the intense ride.

Skylar and Raj had sentineled themselves at the front of the room. They motioned Mark and Teresa to sit at the table; it was clear that they were geared up for a final pitch. Mark braced himself for a hard sell.

"Mark and Teresa, first let me say that Raj and I have been privileged to get to know you. It takes a lot of courage to open up your business and your lives to complete strangers. We want to commend you for your diligence in looking for answers to some of the more challenging questions we threw at you. Teresa, I want to thank you in particular for clearing your calendar these last weeks. I know it cannot have been easy with two busy children. More than that, thanks for making the space for Mark to discover his lead, and then being willing to step back in to the business at a crucial time to co-lead." Skylar seemed softer than usual, bordering on gentle.

Mark looked at Teresa: she seemed to be taking it in. "Don't get snowed, T" he thought to himself.

Raj turned to look deliberately at Mark, square as an Indian doorman at a colonial hotel. "Mark Green. You are an amazing man. I love your ability to take the opposing views of Kris and Whizz and weave them into a stronger fabric. I appreciate your willingness to let them have their voice. Even more, I am greatly psyched to see you discover your own. Three weeks ago I thought you were a 'nice guy' whose talent would enable him to get along in life. Now I see a man of conviction who could, I believe, make a way not driven by market opportunity, but by the call of eternity. You are logical, which is good, but in you I note an emerging truth-tethered leader, so I commend you."

Teresa looked across at Mark to see if he was feeling what she was feeling. They were on opposite sides of the table so she touched him with her eyes. It had been an intense few weeks, and she was feeling a little emotional. The affirmation from Skylar and Raj had an unraveling affect, and her eyes glistened. She wondered whether they noticed.

"Having said this, and fully understanding your decision to embrace the stewardship of the company, we have some recommendations because the roller coaster is about to begin." Skylar clicked on the PowerPoint presentation as she ended her sentence.

Mark heard himself say out loud, to no one in particular, "I was hoping the roller coaster was over."

"That would be nice, Mark, but unlikely. Let me tell you why. But I need some help." She signaled to Raj who left the room saying, "Just a second..." He returned with the old clunker of a bicycle. "Remember this?" he said, flashing his white teeth. "Mark, what do you notice about this bicycle?" he asked in a mock repeat of the earlier conversation.

"Well, Raj, this time I notice it has three handle bars," Mark played along.

"That's very good, Mark. Well done."

Skylar pointed to the Impact Assessment chart. "You will remember the gaps we saw in specific areas such as People and Process. We have concluded that some of this is because of the three handle bars which represent the divergent views on future impact that Kris, Whizz and Mark have. This Purpose-trilemma has caused uncertainty and loss of impact in other areas."

"Mark and Teresa, yesterday we glimpsed the beginnings of a fresh purpose for Green Cycles. This is excellent, and at the same time creates another set of challenges. Simply put, not everyone will agree," Raj said.

"Can you tell us who may not be on board?" Mark asked, not sure if he was asking them to break a confidence.

"Mark," Skylar spoke quietly, "until yesterday, *you* were not on board. It is too soon to tell who will embrace the new Green Cycles. But what we can tell you is you have a unique opportunity to galvanize the company behind a fresh purpose." She looked to the screen as she advanced the slide. "What we heard from you yesterday was something like this:

> The purpose of Green Cycles is to grow a multi-generational community of purpose-driven influencers served by green products and clean business practices so that our footprint on the earth is minimized while our influence for eternity is maximized."

"Here's a slightly different take, Raj offered:

> The purpose of Green Cycles is to serve purpose-driven influencers with green products and a clean business, growing them into a multi-generational community, minimizing the negative footprint on earth while maximizing the positive footprint for eternity."

They watched Mark sit up a little straighter as he read the Purpose statement. "You will need to play with the words," Skylar proceeded, "but when we pushed back on you yesterday, these are the sentiments we heard you express as you defended your position."

"May I ask a question?" Teresa asked. "Why do you use the phrase 'our footprint for eternity is maximized' rather than just speak about God?"

"Good question, Teresa. From what we heard you say yesterday most of your employees and customers may not agree with you in your choice of which god you serve. And some don't even believe in eternity, in the sense of a person dying and going to heaven. But most of them believe there is more to life than just this short stay on earth. Others may even define eternity as a second or third stint on earth. So the wording we have here gives you some room to bring people along in their thinking without being turned off by exclusive-sounding language. Having said that, you must write according to your convictions."

Skylar moved to another slide. "We have three recommendations at this point. First, document your foundational principles, which I believe you have started. Second, have friends test them. Once you have them pretty clear, discuss them will your staff."

"What percentage of the staff has to agree with the principles?" Teresa asked.

"There is no set formula, but the higher up people are in the organization, the more they have to be aligned. And that brings us to another challenge."

The PowerPoint advanced displaying photographs of Mark, Kristoff and Whizz. "How would you describe the worldview of each person, Mark?"

"That is relatively easy... today. A few weeks ago I would not have known. Whizz is a pantheistic environmentalist, Kris is a humanistic atheist, and I am a Christian humanist."

"You are a what?" Skylar asked.

"Well, not that long ago someone told me I was a Christian humanist... Christian in regards to a ticket to heaven, humanist in regards to my business practices. But I am trying to change that."

"Okay," Raj said without passing judgement. "The implication going forward is simple, but not easy: you will need to be clearer on your worldview so that Green Cycles does not get driven off a cliff."

The next slide had a picture of Teresa and another of Kristoff. Skylar asked, "Why do you think we have these pictures up here?"

"Well, we are very different," Teresa offered.

"And you have some similarities," Mark quickly added. "You are both able to get down to brass tacks, and be practical—which is great."

"Teresa, we are no longer in the running to buy your company, so we have no agenda. What, in your view, is the state of your relationship with Kris?"

"I think Kris is a capable person, and I have no doubt he does a good job. He does, after all, have to make sense of Mark and Whizz's non-stop ideas. Having said that, I think he is not in favor of my getting back into the business. That's pretty obvious to me."

"And is it obvious to you, Mark?" Skylar asked.

"No, I did not realize this."

"Mark, how are you going to make a celebrated space for your wife in Green Cycles, and give Kris room to grow? And how are you going to get to the root of Kristoff's need to be in charge? You need to come up with a plan," Skylar advised.

The next slide had a large question mark under the heading, "How do you make decisions?" "You mentioned yesterday that you could not decide to sell without consulting God. If that is correct, then you will have to rethink how you make decisions. Right now, it has a 'mom and pop' feel to it,"

Raj explained. "You will have to decide and document how you will make decisions so that people can participate, and still know your parameters, especially the implications of your new found faith."

"One more thing on this topic," Skylar added, "if you say you want God involved in decision making, you had better get pretty good at getting his input. It will not be as easy as walking to the fridge to take out a juice, but it does need to become a core competence of the company if you are to be 'faith-based.' The principle, based on my research, is that faith comes from hearing the word of God. So you as a company need to be able to hear, listen, and act." She let the point sink in, and could see from their receptivity that this was already something the couple was attuned to.

"Another recommendation before we close things off: Many of your processes are ad hoc, and your annual planning cycle is more like product forecasting than planning. If God is running this business, then we recommend you develop a deliberate approach to planning that starts and ends with God."

"How do we do that?" Mark asked.

"We will leave you with some pointers." Skylar tapped her file indicating there was more there than she was saying aloud.

Raj moved on to another slide with the heading, "How will you measure success?" There was a picture of a redwood tree and a man. "You will need some new measures of success that reflect your purpose. Changed lives are harder to measure than saved trees. So we recommend that you think through what success really is for the new Green Cycles. Mark and Teresa, how would you have described success a month ago? Is it the same today?"

"A month ago I would have said we are successful if customers like the products, they are better for the environment, and staff are happy. Today," Teresa went on, "I am feeling that the main thing that matters is whether God is pleased with us, and would be proud to own this business."

Skylar looked at Raj whose lips seemed pulled across and down at the corners by an invisible ventriloquest. It was his "she's getting it" expression. "Excellent," he said, "Our recommendation is that you build a scorecard that has both immediate and eternal measurements to it."

After a pause, Mark looked at The Duo and asked, "Do you have any other recommendations, personal or business?"

"In fact, we do. Most business leaders in companies your size lack camaraderie. We recommend that you join a business leadership group that caters to both husbands and wives. We checked up and believe Jameson might be able to help you with that."

Skylar handed them a file and said, "Our recommendations are summarized in a memorandum, and the various assessments are in this binder too. Think of them as Wheel Alignment Guidelines: getting everything aligned behind your singluar purpose. We want to wish you well and say we believe the two of you have what it takes to head up a family that makes a lasting difference." She shook Mark's hand, and gave Teresa a hug. As Mark and Teresa walked The Duo towards the reception Skylar said, "And one more thing. Give Stephens & Sanchez a call and tell them it's off, will you?"

"Goodbye, Tamara. Congratulations on passing your graphics test."

"Later," Tamara said, "hey... excuse me... the finals are next week!"

"We know."

Mark and Teresa walked back to his office. As he plopped at his desk and picked up the phone to call S&S, Teresa sat at the small round table. "We will have to get you your own office," he said.

"Not to worry; I like it in here," she smiled and brushed something off her black pashmina shawl. A white feather floated onto the table.

Skylar and Raj flew in to G-D, Inc. to debrief their trip with James, or Big J, as they called him. He was head of acquisitions. They walked down the wide hallway called The Business Hall of Fame. Sketches of corporate leaders, with a brief summary of their achievements, lined the walls. Raj was always inspired by what human beings could achieve, often in tough circumstances. He knew their stories well and ran through them in his mind as he passed their portraits. Abraham—pretty good capital base, but not much of a game plan. Overcame family inertia and finished the job his dad was called to do. Boaz—older guy who took in a young foreign widow, gave her a job, made a happy woman of her. Lydia—spunky woman who supplied the Roman army. Zinzendorf—left a little debt, but did a great job expanding the operation sneaking in all those business missionaries. Carey—battled the odds and changed a nation. "Gotta love these business guys!" Raj said to himself.

He and Skylar sat down with James. Raj thought of Big J as the senior steward of G-D, Inc. who was evidently a great manager in his day. James gave them a hearty hug. "So, how was the assignment? Was it successful?"

"I think so," Skylar said, "although it was touch and go at times."

He spread his arms and said, "We have plenty of 'time', and you know I like a good story..."

"Okay. The first challenge was getting Stephens & Sanchez to accept our terms. Clearly they were out of their league, but they accepted the Memorandum of Understanding, then pretty much backed off."

"They didn't want to know who the buyer was?"

"They did, but we told them it was classified." Raj said.

"The next problem?" Big J asked.

"Actually, we didn't have much spiritual capital to work with because there weren't too many people praying for Green, poor guy. His wife,

Teresa, thought her husband was spiritually anemic, but she had no complaints because he was an all round nice guy."

"How did you fix that? Did you make her disgruntled?"

Skylar had been on point for this piece of the assignment, so she shared the details. "Vera, the model mother-in-law, was the key. We popped an idea in her head about Mark having a bit of a midlife crisis, and this got her concerned for her daughter. So she went to her pastor and her women's prayer group. She fed just enough information to a few key people, and the word spread rapidly among the galloping grannies."

"Good job—any snags?"

"Actually there was," Raj jumped in. "Joe, Vera's husband, was pretty adamant that she should stay out of it, so I got him invited on a fishing trip with some of his old buddies."

Skylar continued, "With him out of cell phone range Vera had free rein and nearly took Mark to the cleaners. There was a brilliant meeting where she gave him the silk glove, steel hand ultimatum. She pretty much said, 'You listen to and work with my daughter or I won't sign off on the sale.' For me, it was one highlight of the assignment."

"By this stage Mark had gone from being the 'in control CEO' to being the 'I just let the tiger out the bag' due diligence subject. On the home front not only had Vera been adamant, but Teresa was rediscovering her passion for the business. She started wondering what it would be like if she actually exercised her rights as a shareholder. The crescendo was when poor Mark nearly choked on his meal as she nonchalantly threw out that she owned 65% of the corporation. It wasn't strictly true, but Mark was in no position to start an argument since Vera had made it clear that Mark and Teresa had to be a team. If Teresa so much as breathed to Vera that Mark was being a bozo, the deal was dead."

"And how's our man Jameson doing down there? Is he managing to stay under the radar?"

"For the most part, but not completely. When Vera and crew started praying for Mark to have an encounter with a godly business guy, we opted to make a way for Ken to speak at the church Mark and Teresa attend..."

"Not that often..." Raj interrupted Skylar's story.

"Teresa told Mark they needed some guidance and he obliged—he didn't have much choice since Vera had been on his case just the day before. They went to the Sunday service and Ken told the old donkey story."

"Ass, asset... I like that one," said James.

"Mark was pretty touched, I would say, and even took some notes about why God needed his business, but we figured he might forget most of it by Monday, so we kept the fire going in Vera."

"'Your son-in-law needs to speak to this man,' we whispered about 20 times during the sermon. Well, hurricane Vera made a beeline for Ken afterwards and made him commit to reaching out to Mark."

"Did he do it?"

"He sure did, although he didn't have much time, and he nearly rubbed Mark the wrong way when he went straight for the throat and told him he was a Christian Humanist."

"What did Mark think?"

"He didn't know enough about humanists to be offended, and he was more surprised Ken had thrown in the Christian part. But the encounter got Mark's attention, and Ken gave him a homework assignment."

"What was it?"

"He had to come up with a Bible verse to support each category of his business philosophy. Since Mark had latched onto The 10-Ps, all he needed to do was find 10 scriptures."

"Good strategy on Ken's part. Did Mark do it?"

"He got an 'A' for effort, but let's just say he is still working on the content. Ken has plans to pull Mark into a president's council. So he will learn."

"Any other hurdles?"

"There were a small pile of obstacles, starting with the fact that Mark didn't know Jesus from Adam. What was great about his situation was how Ken used the obviously different worldviews of a couple of Mark's managers to underline the fact that Mark was at sixes and sevens. Mark had some pretty good didactic reasoning, however, and saw the huge implications of God getting his hands on someone's business. So when he got back together with Ken it all led to a 'Jesus, meet my friend, Mark' conversation that was precious."

Skylar agreed, "It was probably the best part. Raj and I popped right out and had a party. But the other thing that was an obstacle was Teresa: I am not sure how well prepared she was for Mark's turnaround. More people need to pray for the wives so that they are on board with their husband's new enthusiasm."

"We'll make a note," James smiled, as if she were saying something new.

"Vera could have been a problem, along the same lines," Raj explained. "These folks on earth seem to have a habit of praying, but not being ready for the answer when it comes. She was a little suspicious when Mark went back and said they had decided not to sell."

Skylar looked pensive. "James, there was one more test thrown at Mark and Teresa that nearly shook them. The counter offer from S&S with the big price tag—Mammon nearly got the better of them. Why was it allowed so soon?"

"You two know the principle: after the blessing comes the testing. It's not a law, but it helps to solidify the truth. We faced a few dangers after Mark's conversion. The first was that he didn't know enough to draft decent foundational principles, let alone go toe to toe with Kris and Whizz. The second danger was Mark and Teresa needed some team practice, and this was not a decision they could take to others. They had to wrestle it to the mat themselves, so it gave them a ready opportunity to build spiritual muscle. The third reason for the test is business leaders have to face Mammon at some point. Greed is the fall of many who say they follow Jesus, but are really following the money. It was their biggest test, and, thankfully, they passed."

Raj and Skylar filled Big J in on some more details, and then he asked one more question. "How was the session when Mark and Teresa told you they were no longer interested in selling? I would like to have seen your faces."

"We had to be careful because there were a few times when we did or said things that could have made them suspicious," Skylar started,

"Like your feather pin, Skylar—you have to think about leaving that behind next time!" Raj teased Skylar.

"Well, there was more than one occasion when you let out information no one told us, remember?" Skylar retorted.

"So much had happened in a few weeks that we had to remain pretty low key in the "no go" meeting. We wanted to jump up and down, hug them, explain everything to them. Instead we made them sweat a little, like they had done us a huge inconvenience, and we asked the normal, 'and you are sure about this?' questions. We pushed back to test their commitment and thinking, but they were pretty solid. We were totally stoked."

"Stoked, Raj?"

"Yes, that's what we get when in California, James... stoked!"

"Sum up your highlights for me, Skylar." James looked at her.

"For me it was some of the standard items, but I never tire of seeing them. Mark and Teresa learning deeper collaboration in the business—such a picture of what we have here—that was a highlight for me. Vera and the old ducks at the church getting into the game—they made the difference and re-enforced that there is no such thing as retirement. I would have to say, though, that Teresa and Mark's decision to embrace a long term, multi-generational calling for the business to be a platform for extending the kingdom, and their willingness to not forego their true calling for some immediate cash—that was probably the pinnacle."

"How about you, Raj—what were your high points?"

"I genuinely liked my interactions with Whizz and Kris and Tamara and others at Green Cycles. They are sincere people and some of them had a better sense of their identity than Mark did when we started. The Mark/Ken encounters were priceless. Ken didn't just get him 'saved', as they like to say, but he enlisted him in the Master's cause. I have to say, while the encounters were great, the early steps of growth and re-laying the foundations were just as important to me. To see them get a new appetite for truth and to understand the issue of alignment was incredible. Also, the heightened awareness to things that have yet to be reconciled to Truth is encouraging. So, in summary, I liked the quick but solid implementation steps. They are not glamorous, but they show commitment."

"Skylar, Raj—well done! We are proud of you back here at G-D, Inc. We have another company in the G-D, Inc. portfolio and a new husband-wife team in the President's Club. Maybe they will become Kingdom Business Hall of Famers like your heroes out there."

Big J paused to look at a folder in front of him. "Are you ready for your next assignment?"

"Sure, where to now?"

"Indonesia!"

"And our roles for this assignment?"

"Let me see: you, Skylar, are going to be a businessman from Sweden, and you, Raj, are going to be a South African pastor-turned-leadership coach."

"No feathers this time, Skylar."

"And no heavenly-gem cufflinks for you."

Skylar inquired, "Is it another person wanting to sell their household?"

"No. There is a good businessman with a rather large sphere of influence who is about to close up shop so that he can 'go into ministry,'" James explained.

"Oh, brother."

THE END

Listing of historical people, corporations and trademarks

Airbook
Apple
Arthur Guinness
Asa Candler
Cadbury's
Cardica
Coca-Cola
Correct Craft
Edison Electric
Facebook
Gary Fisher
Guinness
JC Penny
Joe Breeze
Nike
Odwalla Juice
Peet's Coffee
Quaker Oats
Service Master
Starbucks Coffee
Thomas Edison
Tom Ritchey
Toyota
Twitter
Volkswagen
Winston Churchill

About the Author

He and his wife, Lyn, founded a Silicon Valley Think Tank called The Institute for Innovation, Integration & Impact in 1996. Brett and Lyn and a growing community of Institute-trained associates have repurposed hundreds of companies around the world.

He and his wife, Lyn, live in Saratoga, California. They have three grown children, Fay Maree, James Brett who is married to Jessica, and David Iain.

End note:
Scripture references have been omitted. Feel free to contact the author if you would like to know the source.